Name ____________________

MW00721262

10	10	67	67	10
+ 7	+ 27	+ 10	+ 10	+ 97

$\square + 82 = 92$

$10 + \square = 35$

15	6	72
+ 28	8	+ 39
	7	
	5	
	3	
	4	
	+ 2	

121	15
+ 220	90
	+ 35

$17 + \square + 10 = 37$

$20 + 9 = \square$

$10 + 9 = \square$

$5 + 9 + 6 + 8 + 4 = \square$

©1964 Lore Rasmussen

Ref: *Lab Sheet Annotations*, page 52.

Name ______________________ Date ______________

4 3 + 7	88 + 10	88 + 20

10
8
4
+ 6

8 + 5 = ☐

45
+ 8

19
+ 6

45 + ☐ = 100

15
35
35
+ 15

155
+ 145

25 + 25 = ☐

25
25
+ 25

82
+ 18

25 + 25 + 25 + 25 = ☐

©1964 Lore Rasmussen

Ref: *Lab Sheet Annotations,* page 52.

Name ______________________ Date ______________

1. How big are the jumps?

24 → 59 □

84 → 102 □

32 → 60 □

56 → 63 □

62 → 64 □

56 → 93 □

2. Where did we start?

□ —8→ 29

□ —18→ 104

□ —18→ 42

□ —8→ 112

□ —28→ 42

□ —5→ 86

□ —7→ 63

□ —14→ 75

□ —17→ 73

□ —3→ 186

□ —38→ 129

□ —25→ 36

©1964 Lore Rasmussen

Ref: *Lab Sheet Annotations*, page 63.

Name ______________________ Date ______________________

$$\begin{array}{r} 23 \\ -\ 7 \\ \hline \square \end{array} \qquad \begin{array}{r} 26 \\ -\ 8 \\ \hline \square \end{array} \qquad \begin{array}{r} 34 \\ -\ 8 \\ \hline \square \end{array} \qquad \begin{array}{r} 35 \\ -\ 6 \\ \hline \square \end{array}$$

$$\begin{array}{r} \square \\ +\ 7 \\ \hline 23 \end{array} \qquad \begin{array}{r} \square \\ +\ 8 \\ \hline 26 \end{array} \qquad \begin{array}{r} \square \\ +\ 8 \\ \hline 34 \end{array} \qquad \begin{array}{r} \square \\ +\ 6 \\ \hline 35 \end{array}$$

$34 - 8 = \square$

$34 + 7 = \square$

$$\begin{array}{r} 40 \\ -\ 5 \\ \hline \square \end{array} \qquad \begin{array}{r} 34 \\ -\ 17 \\ \hline \square \end{array}$$

$48 + \square = 50$

$58 + \square = 61$

$34 + \square = 54$

$\square + 5 = 25$

$$\begin{array}{r} 61 \\ -\ 58 \\ \hline \square \end{array} \qquad \begin{array}{r} \square \\ -\ 5 \\ \hline 40 \end{array}$$

©1964 Lore Rasmussen

Name ________________________ Date ________________

Look at this picture. It is your clue.

3 cups of 2 blocks $\overset{b}{=}$ 2 cups of 3 blocks

Get real blocks and cups to help finish the next problems.

4 cups of 3 blocks $\overset{b}{=}$ 3 cups of ☐ blocks

5 cups of 2 blocks $\overset{b}{=}$ 2 cups of ☐ blocks

5 cups of ☐ blocks $\overset{b}{=}$ 4 cups of 5 blocks

©1964 Lore Rasmussen

Ref: *Lab Sheet Annotations*, pages 108 and 127.

Name ______________________ Date ______________

Check your answers with real cups and blocks

3 cups of 7 blocks $\overset{b}{=}$ 7 cups of $\square$ blocks

6 cups of 5 blocks $\overset{b}{=}$ 5 cups of $\square$ blocks

5 cups of $\square$ blocks $\overset{b}{=}$ 1 cup of 5 blocks

4 cups of 6 blocks $\overset{b}{=}$ 6 cups of $\square$ blocks

9 cups of 3 blocks $\overset{b}{=}$ 3 cups of $\square$ blocks

2 cups of $\square$ blocks $\overset{b}{=}$ 8 cups of 2 blocks

©1964 Lore Rasmussen

Ref: *Lab Sheet Annotations*, page 108.

Name ______________________________ Date ____________________

3 X 4 units = ☐ units — 3 X 4 = ☐

3 X 4 tens = ☐ tens — 3 X 40 = ☐

3 X 4 hundreds = ☐ hundreds — 3 X 400 = ☐

---

5 X 3 units = ☐ units — 5 X 3 = ☐

5 X 3 tens = ☐ tens — 5 X 30 = ☐

5 X 3 hundreds = ☐ hundreds — 5 X 300 = ☐

---

6 X 3 units = ☐ units — 6 X 3 = ☐

6 X 3 tens = ☐ tens — 6 X 30 = ☐

6 X 3 hundreds = ☐ hundreds — 6 X 300 = ☐

---

5 X 2	50 X 2	500 X 2	Make up your own problems.
4 X 6	40 X 6	400 X 6	
3 X 7	30 X 7	300 X 7	

©1964 Lore Rasmussen

Ref: *Lab Sheet Annotations*, page 128.

Name ______________________ Date ______________________

3 X 2 =

3 X 20 =

3 X 5 =

30 X 5 =

7 X 5 =

7 X 50 =

7 X 4 =

7 X 40 =

9 X 1 =

90 X 1 =

6 X 10 =

6 X 100 =

3 X 6 =

3 X 60 =

3 X 600 =

8 X 4 =

8 X 40 =

8 X 400 =

5 X 6 =

50 X 6 =

500 X 6 =

7 X 6 =

7 X 60 =

7 X 600 =

13 X 2 =

13 X 20 =

13 X 200 =

5 X 15 =

50 X 15 =

500 X 15 =

8 X 60 =

30 X 12 =

50 X 9 =

6 X 400 =

8 X 800 =

600 X 9 =

©1964 Lore Rasmussen

Ref: *Lab Sheet Annotations*, page 128.

Name________________________ Date______________

How many 3's in 12 ? ______
How many 4's in 12 ? ______

12 ÷ 3 =
12 ÷ 4 =

$3\overline{)12}$ $4\overline{)12}$

How many 9's in 18 ? ______
How many 2's in 18 ? ______

18 ÷ 9 =
18 ÷ 2 =

$9\overline{)18}$ $2\overline{)18}$

How many 4's in 16? ______

16 ÷ 4 =

$4\overline{)16}$

How many 4's in 20 ? ______
How many 5's in 20 ? ______

20 ÷ 4 =
20 ÷ 5 =

$4\overline{)20}$ $5\overline{)20}$

How many 8's in 24 ? ______
How many 3's in 24 ? ______

24 ÷ 8 =
24 ÷ 3 =

$8\overline{)24}$ $3\overline{)24}$

©1964 Lore Rasmussen
Ref: *Lab Sheet Annotations*, page 179.

Name________________________________ Date________________________

Four Ways to Write About the Same Thing

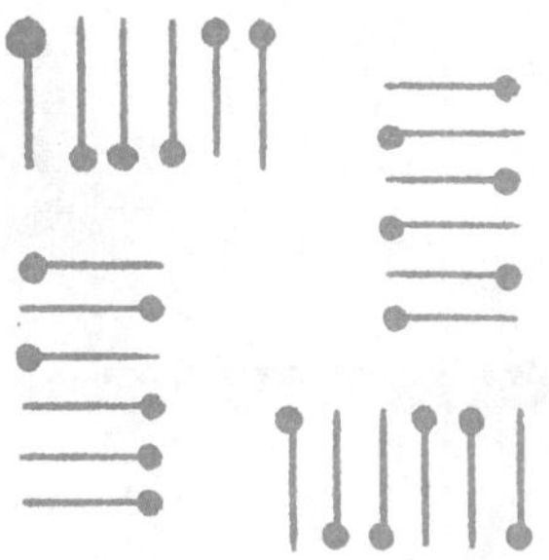

24 pins divided

into groups of 6.

How many groups ?

24 ÷ 6 = (4)

24 = ○ X 6

6)24 (quotient: ○)

$\frac{24}{6}$ = ○

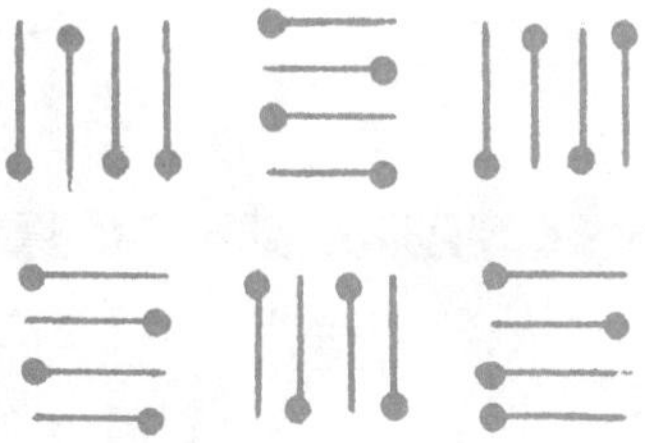

Write in four ways about this picture.

□ ← pins

△ ← in each group

○ ← groups

① □ ÷ △ = ○

② □ = ○ X △

③ △)□ (quotient: ○)

④ $\frac{□}{△}$ = ○

©1964 Lore Rasmussen

Ref: *Lab Sheet Annotations*, page 179.

Name ______________________ Date ______________

	÷ 5		X 5	
45	→	○	→	□
30	→	○	→	□
25	→	○	→	□
15	→	○	→	□
35	→	○	→	□
40	→	○	→	□
50	→	○	→	□
20	→	○	→	□
5	→	○	→	□

©1964 Lore Rasmussen

Ref: *Lab Sheet Annotations*, page 181.

Name ______________________ Date ______________

45 —÷ 9→ ○ —X 9→ □

30 —÷ 6→ ○ —X 6→ □

25 —÷ 5→ ○ —X 5→ □

15 —÷ 3→ ○ —X 3→ □

35 —÷ 7→ ○ —X 7→ □

40 —÷ 8→ ○ —X 8→ □

50 —÷ 10→ ○ —X 10→ □

20 —÷ 4→ ○ —X 4→ □

5 —÷ 1→ ○ —X 1→ □

©1964 Lore Rasmussen

Ref: *Lab Sheet Annotations*, page 181.

Name ______________________ Date ______________________

$5\overline{)25}$	$5\overline{)30}$	$5\overline{)35}$	$5\overline{)40}$
$5 \times \square = 25$	$5 \times \square = 30$	$5 \times \square = 35$	$5 \times \square = 40$

$45 \div 5 = \square$	$50 \div 5 = \square$	$55 \div 5 = \square$
$\square \times 5 = 45$	$50 = \square \times 5$	$55 = 5 \times \square$

$15 \xrightarrow{\div 5} \bigcirc \xrightarrow{\times 5} \square$

$4 \xrightarrow{\times 5} \text{hexagon} \xrightarrow{\div 5} \bigtriangledown$

$\frac{1}{1} = \square$ $\frac{2}{2} = \square$ $\frac{3}{3} = \square$ $\frac{4}{4} = \square$

$\frac{5}{5} = \square$ $\frac{10}{5} = \square$ $\frac{15}{5} = \square$ $\frac{20}{5} = \square$

$5 \times \frac{1}{5} = \square$ $10 \times \frac{1}{5} = \square$

©1964 Lore Rasmussen

Ref: *Lab Sheet Annotations*, page 181.

Name________________________ Date______________

Find the "tricky" names for 6.

Make up some more of your own.

$30 \div 5$

$2\overline{)12}$

$\frac{12}{2}$

6

$3\overline{)18}$

$\frac{6}{1}$

$24 \div 4$

$10\overline{)60}$

$36 \div 6$

$7\overline{)42}$

$6 \times \frac{6}{6}$

©1964 Lore Rasmussen

Name ______________________ Date ______________

Make up some more problems like these.

$1 < \square < 3$

$9 < \square < 11$

$\frac{1}{3}$ of $9 = \square = \frac{1}{2} \times 6$

$4 > \square > 0$

$99 < \square < 109$

$1\frac{1}{2} > \square > \frac{1}{2}$

$\frac{1}{3} < \square < \frac{3}{4}$

$6 \times 6 > \square > 4 \times 6$

$16 \div 2 > \square > 16 \div 4$

©1964 Lore Rasmussen

Ref: *Lab Sheet Annotations*, page 204.

Name______________________________ Date______________________

True or False ?

$6+2 = 4+4$	T F
$9-3 = 5+2$	T F
$11-1 = 10-2$	T F
$11-3 = 10-2$	T F
$6+8 = 7+7$	T F
$15-6 = 10-1$	T F
$3 \times 3 = 3+6$	T F
$5 \times 4 = (4 \times 4)+4$	T F
$9-3 = 10-4$	T F
$6+6 = 5+8$	T F
$9+7 = 2 \times 8$	T F
$3+5 = 2 \times 5$	T F
$100+100 = 200$	T F
$20 + 20 = 10+31$	T F
$60 > (5 \times 10)+11$	T F
$34 < 17+17$	T F
	T F
	T F

Name______________________________Date________________________

I WOULD RATHER HAVE:

(4 X 3) balloons or 10 balloons

(7 X 10) pennies or half a dollar

$5\frac{1}{2}$ candy bars or ($\frac{1}{2}$ X 10) candy bars

$\frac{1}{2}$ dozen eggs or 6 eggs

(5 X 5) marbles or 2 dozen marbles

$\frac{1}{3}$ of 30 arrowheads or $\frac{1}{2}$ of 20 arrowheads

(4 X 4)+ 1 gum drops or (2 X 9)-1 gum drops

$\frac{1}{6}$ of a cake or $\frac{1}{3}$ of a cake

($\frac{1}{4}$ X 100) garnets or 20 garnets

©1964 Lore Rasmussen

Ref: *Lab Sheet Annotations*, page 204.

Name____________________ Date________________

I would rather have

(3×2) wormy apples	or	$(\frac{1}{5} \times 20)$ wormy apples
40 pennies	or	(3×3) nickles
$(\frac{1}{2} \times 50)$ marbles	or	$(9 \times 3) - 2$ marbles
$(7 \times 4) - 2$ bees	or	$(5 \times 4) - 7$ bees
$\frac{1}{5}$ of a dollar	or	$\frac{1}{4}$ of a dollar
$(119 \times \frac{1}{2})$ balloons	or	$(3 \times 6) - 1$ balloons
$(\frac{1}{2} \times 8)$ cookies	or	$(\frac{1}{4} \times 100) - 21$ cookies
(13×2) frogs	or	$\frac{1}{2} \times 50$ frogs

P.S. I would rather have one nose than three noses, even though one is less than three

©1964 Lore Rasmussen

Ref: *Lab Sheet Annotations*, page 204.

Name ______________________ Date ______________________

These are "open sentences" <u>waiting</u> to be made true.	Which of these will make the sentence true? Put loops around the number names that will work.
$8 > \square > 4$	$9,\ 8\frac{1}{2},\ 8,\ 7\frac{1}{2},\ 7,\ 6\frac{1}{2},\ 6,\ 5,\ 4\frac{1}{2}$
$104 < 109 < \square$	190, 140, 110, 107, 100
$1010 > \square > 1001$	1000, 2006, 999, 1007
$3 > 6 - 8 > \square$	1, 0, -1, -2, -3, -4
$\square > 1 > 0$	$-5,\ 2,\ 107,\ 25,\ -2,\ 1\frac{1}{2}$
$\square < \frac{1}{4} < \frac{1}{3}$	$\frac{1}{2},\ \frac{1}{5},\ 1,\ 2,\ \frac{1}{9},\ \frac{1}{100}$

©1964 Lore Rasmussen

Ref: *Lab Sheet Annotations*, page 204.

Name________________________ Date________________

$1 > \square$

$\square > 45$

$9 < \square$

$6 - 2 > \square$

$3 \times 3 \times 3 > \square$

$6 \div 3 > \square$

$\square < 11$

$\square > 5$

$\square > 10 - 3 - 3$

$9 > \square > \square$

$\square > (6 \times 10) + 3$

$10 - 1 > \square$

$3 \times 5 \neq \square$

$34 < 17 + 17$	T	F
$60 > (5 \times 10) + 11$	T	F
$6 \div 3 > 6 - 3$	T	F
$6 \times 5 \neq (3 \times 5) + (3 \times 5)$	T	F
$221 > 212$	T	F
$-7 > -5$	T	F
$10 \div 10 \neq 0$	T	F
$10 - 10 \neq 0$	T	F
$6 \times 2 > \frac{1}{2} \times 24$	T	F
$6 \times \frac{1}{2} \neq \frac{1}{2} \times 6$	T	F
$\frac{1}{2} \times 40 < \frac{1}{2} \times 50$	T	F
$(2 \times 4) - 3 - 2 > 1$	T	F

Name ______________________ Date ______________

TABLE

PICTURE	❒	□	|	•
A		4	4	8
B				
C				
D				
E				
F				
G				
H				

A

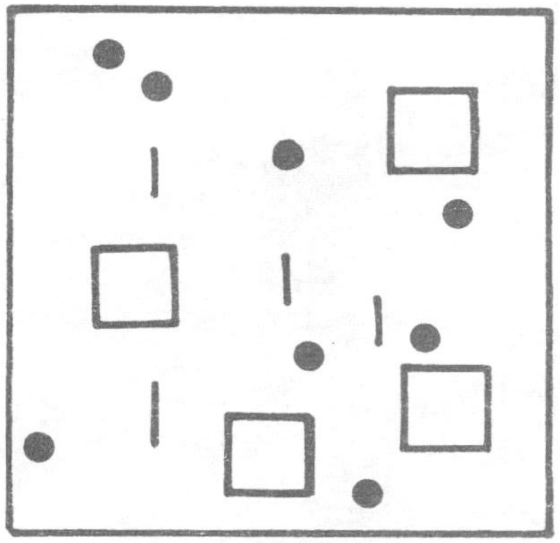

B

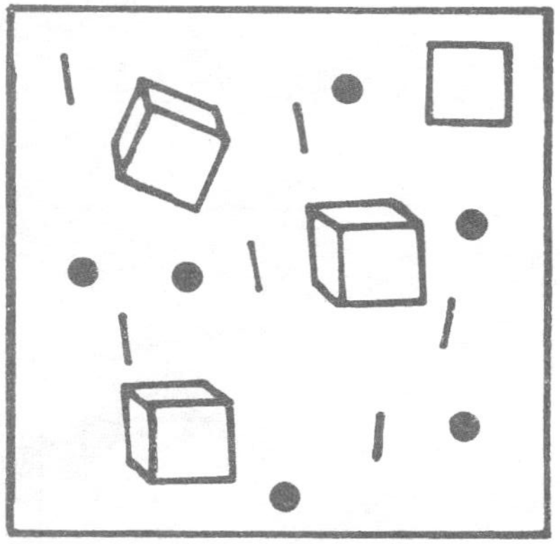

C

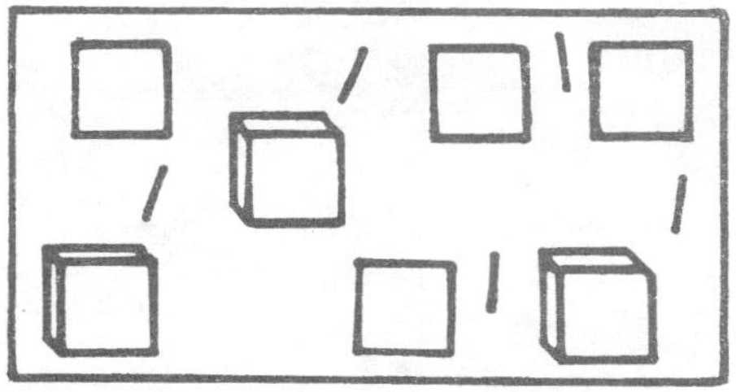

D

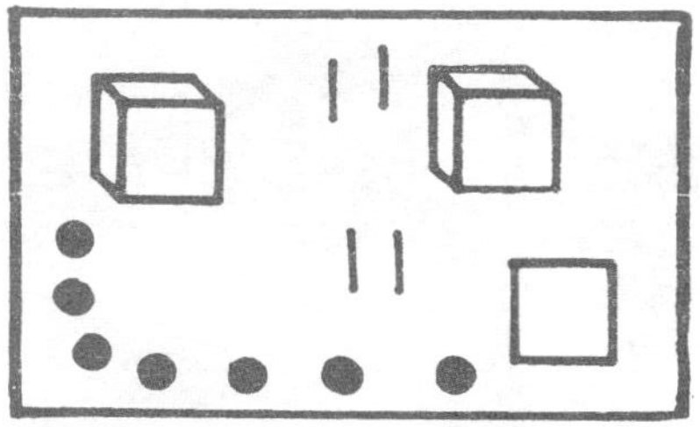

E

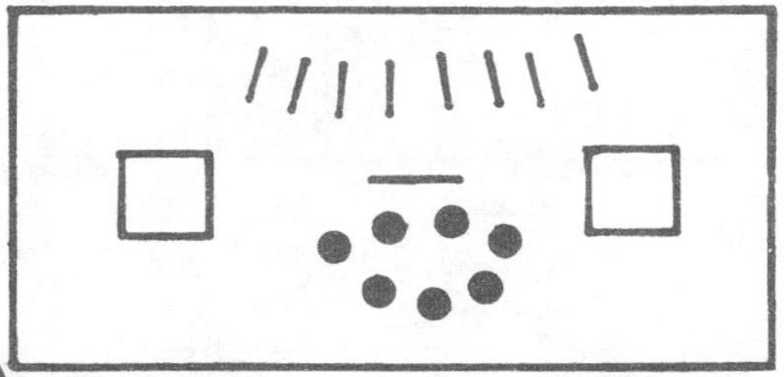

F

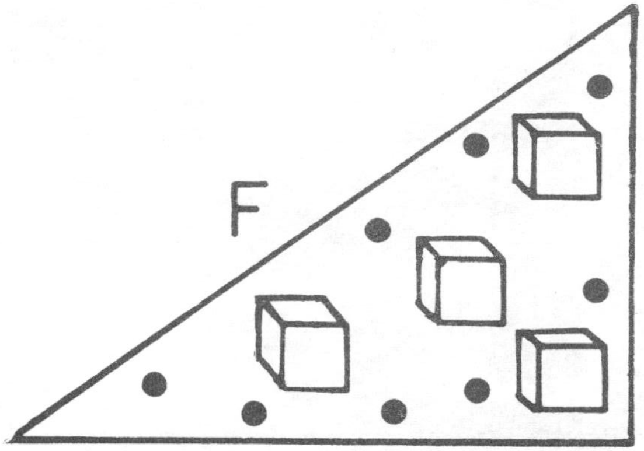

G

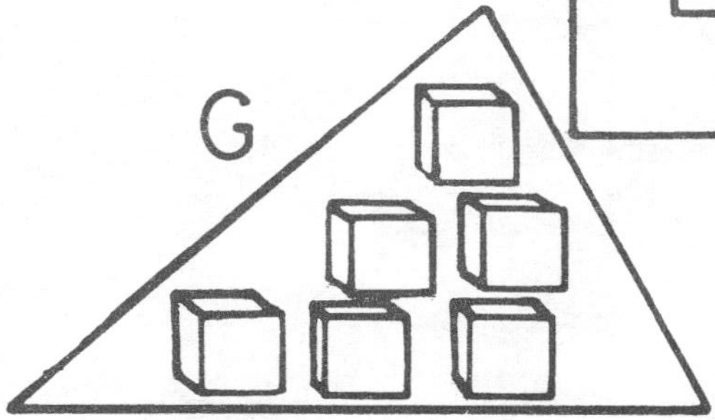

H

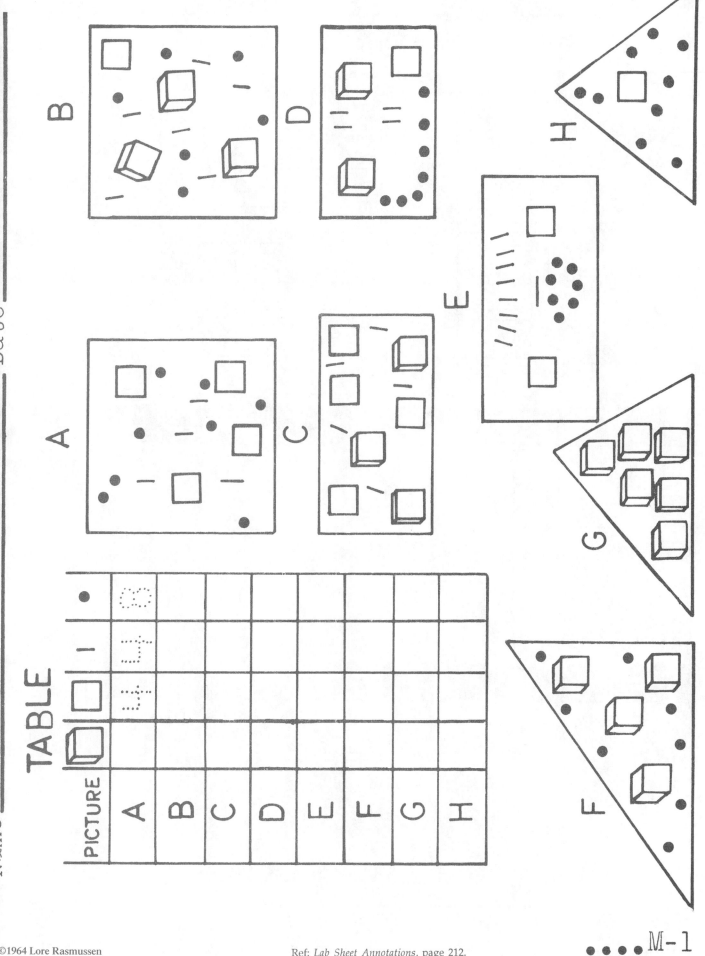

©1964 Lore Rasmussen

Ref: *Lab Sheet Annotations*, page 212.

Name______________________________ Date________________________

Table

picture	1000	100	10	1
A	3	2	3	7
B				
C				
D				
E				
F				
G				
H				

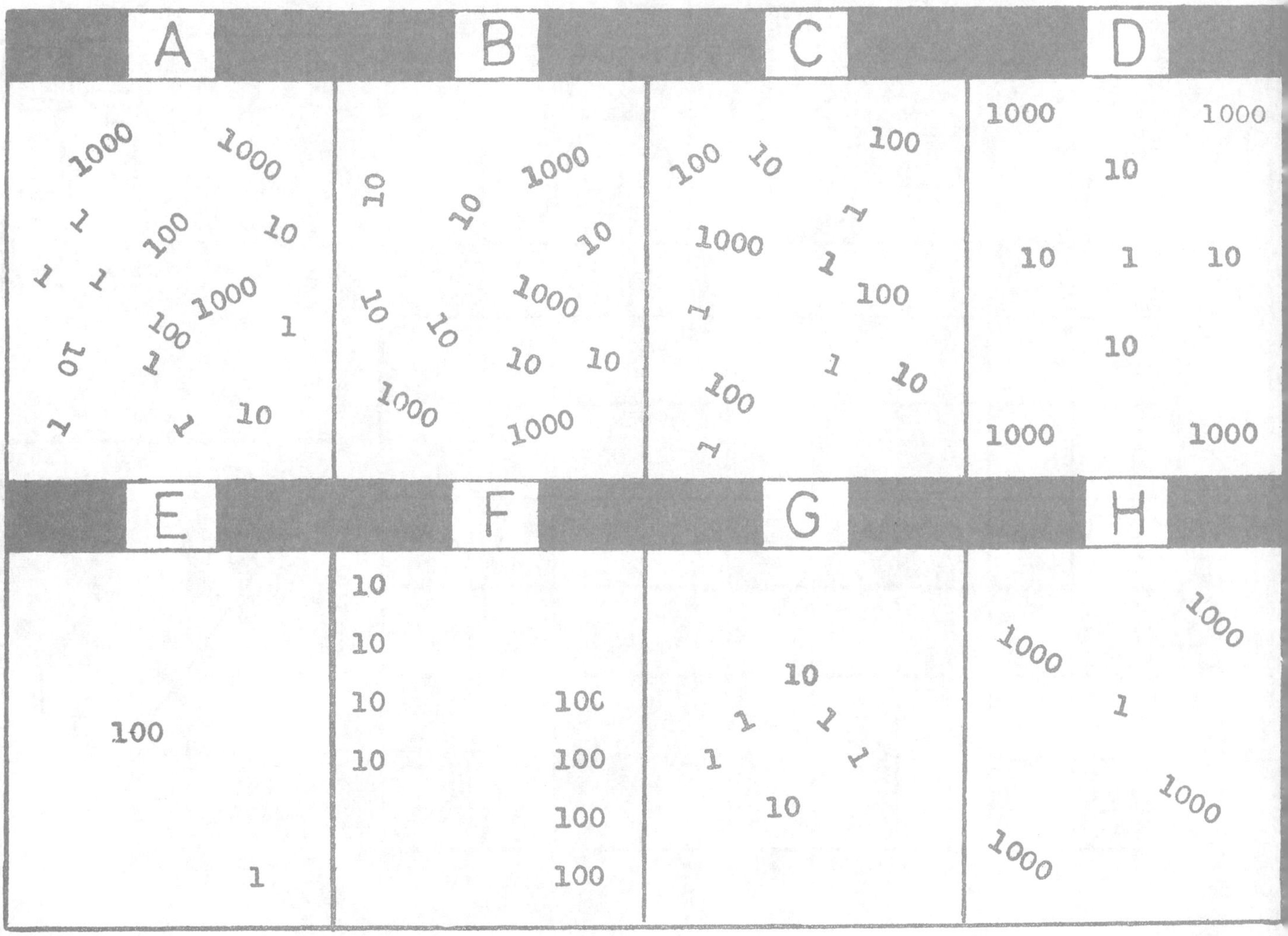

©1964 Lore Rasmussen

Ref: *Lab Sheet Annotations*, page 212.

Name____________________ Date ____________________

TABLE

PICTURE	Th	H	T	U
A				
B				
C				
D				
E				
F				
G				
H				

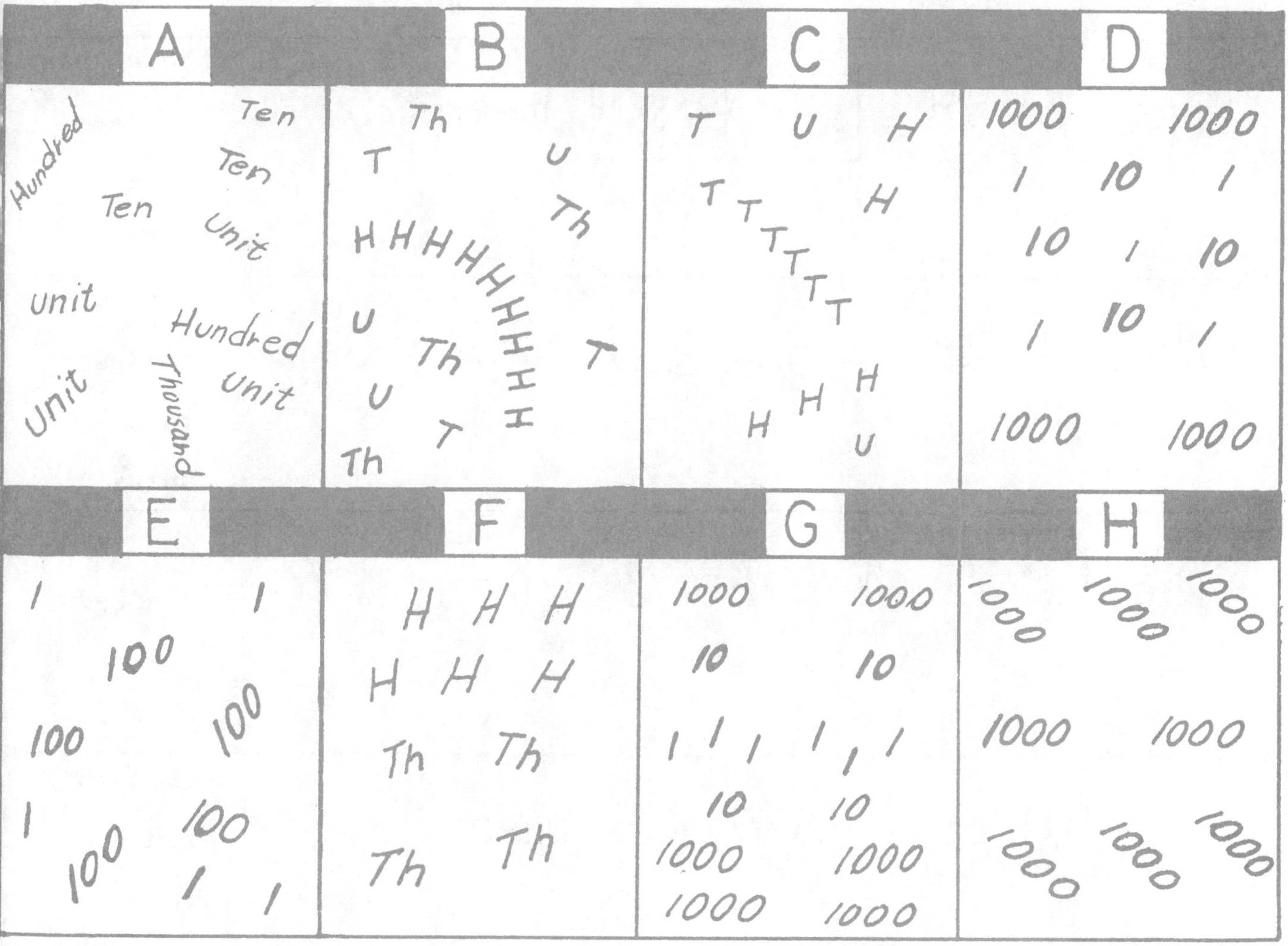

©1964 Lore Rasmussen

Ref: *Lab Sheet Annotations*, page 212.

Name ______________________ Date ______________

Th	H	T	U
	6	3	5

The '5' in 635 means 5 — thousands / hundreds / tens / units (example: 5 is joined to "units")

Th	H	T	U
2	7	0	4

The '7' in 2704 means 7 — thousands / hundreds / tens / units

---

Th	H	T	U
	5	7	6

The '7' in 576 means 7 — thousands / hundreds / tens / units

Th	H	T	U
		3	2

The '3' in 32 means 3 — thousands / hundreds / tens / units

The '3' in 3420 means 3 — thousands / hundreds / tens / units

---

The '8' in 608 means 8 — thousands / hundreds / tens / units

The '0' in 5083 means 0 — thousands / hundreds / tens / units

©1964 Lore Rasmussen

Ref: *Lab Sheet Annotations*, page 214.

Name ______________________ Date ______________________

Th	H	T	U		
	3	5	8	=	50 + 300 + 8
				=	500 + 400 + 9 + 90
				=	4000 + 80 + 600 + 1
				=	700 + 3 + 200 + 30
				=	20 + 5 + 3 + 600
				=	60 + 100 + 30
				=	50 + 5000 + 4000 + 100 + 30
				=	600 + 300 + 4 + 5
				=	8000 + 1 + 10 + 80

©1964 Lore Rasmussen

Name________________________ Date________________

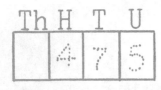

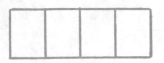

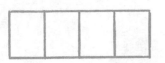

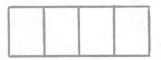

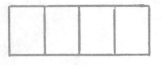

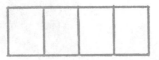

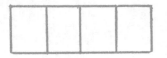

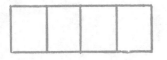

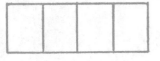

Th	H	T	U	
	4	7	5	4 hundreds + 7 tens + 5 units
				8 hundreds + 2 tens + 3 units
				6 hundreds + 0 tens + 6 units
				2 hundreds + 5 tens + 0 units
				8 hundreds + 9 tens
				5 hundreds + 3 units
				4 thousands + 7 hundreds + 2 tens + 1 unit
				1 thousand + 7 tens + 6 units
				0 thousands + 7 units + 0 tens

©1964 Lore Rasmussen

Ref: *Lab Sheet Annotations*, page 214.

Name ______________________ Date ______________

40 + 20	3 + 5	43 + 25
20 + 50	7 + 2	27 + 52

100 + 400	30 + 60	5 + 2	135 + 462
500 + 200	40 + 40	3 + 2	543 + 242

©1964 Lore Rasmussen

Ref: *Lab Sheet Annotations*, page 215.

Name ______________ Date ______________

```
  24      63      50      44
+ 51    + 34    + 47    + 55
----    ----    ----    ----
```

```
  347       657       545
+ 532     + 231     + 432
-----     -----     -----
```

```
  716       405       357
+ 182     + 503     + 243
-----     -----     -----
```

```
  232
  323         0123456789
  121       + 9876543210
+ 212       ------------
-----
```

©1964 Lore Rasmussen

Ref: *Lab Sheet Annotations*, page 215.

Name ______________________ Date ______________

1000 = [ ] thousand

1000 = [ ] hundreds

1000 = [ ] tens

1000 = [ ] units

100 = [ ] hundred

100 = [ ] tens

100 = [ ] units

10 = [ ] ten

10 = [ ] units

1 = [ ] unit

©1964 Lore Rasmussen

Ref: *Lab Sheet Annotations*, page 217.

Name ____________________ Date ______________

13 units = 1 ten + [3] units

17 units = 1 ten + □ units

11 units = 1 ten + □ unit

19 units = □ tens + 9 units

10 units = 1 ten + □ units

18 tens = 1 hundred + □ tens

14 tens = 1 hundred + □ tens

25 tens = □ hundreds + 5 tens

12 tens = 1 hundred + □ tens

16 hundreds = 1 thousand + □ hundreds

16 tens = 1 hundred + □ tens

16 units = 1 ten + □ units

13 hundreds = 1 thousand + □ hundreds

©1964 Lore Rasmussen

Ref: *Lab Sheet Annotations*, page 217.

Name ______________________ Date ______________

3 units + 5 units = ☐ units

0 units + 7 units = ☐ units

4 tens + 2 tens = ☐ tens

6 hundreds + 3 hundreds = ☐ hundreds

5 tens + 7 tens = ☐ tens

5 tens + 7 tens = 1 hundred + ☐ tens

6 units + 9 units = ☐ units

6 units + 9 units = 1 ten + ☐ units

7 units + 7 units = 1 ten + ☐ units

9 tens + 4 tens = ☐ hundreds + 3 tens

6 units + 6 units = 1 ten + ☐ units

5 tens + 8 tens = 1 hundred + ☐ tens

9 tens + 7 tens = 1 hundred + ☐ tens

8 units + 8 units = 1 ten + ☐ units

©1964 Lore Rasmussen

Ref: *Lab Sheet Annotations*, page 217.

Name ______________________ Date ______________________

Th	H	T	U		Th	H	T	U
	8	3	14	=		8	4	4
	2	6	12	=		2		2
	5	13	4	=			3	4
1	6	0	11	=	1	6		1
7	13	4	17	=	8	3		7

	7	1	23	=		7		13	=		7		3
5	3	9	13	=	5	3		3	=	5		0	3
2	9	10	0	=	2		0	0	=		0	0	0

7	9	9	12	=	7	9		2	=	7		0	2	=		0	0	2

©1964 Lore Rasmussen

Name ______________________ Date ______________

```
  708        462        137
+ 156      + 376      + 137
  8 5 14
  864

  875        637       7421
+ 119      + 350     +  859

  296       3044        325
+ 157     + 2258        134
                        207
                      + 222

    537429021
  + 462570978
```

Name ________________ Date ____________

```
  547      463      905
+ 234    + 463    +  67
-----    -----    -----

  888      467      642
+  22    + 298    + 983
-----    -----    -----

  56284      125      99
+ 34816      642      88
-------      753      77
           + 945    + 66
           -----    ----
```

©1964 Lore Rasmussen

Ref: *Lab Sheet Annotations*, page 217.

page 4

	6	4								7	7
+	5	9			4	7	6		+	7	7
				+	9	6	4				
	3	6								1	4
+	6	8								3	7
					6	6				6	1
					7	7				5	4
				+	8	8			+	2	3

fold here

page 1

MY FIFTH LITTLE MATH BOOK

Name ____________________

Date ____________________

©1964 Lore Rasmussen

Ref: *Lab Sheet Annotations*, page 217.

page 2

	5	7				4	6				
+	3	2			+	3	3				
				4	4					7	2
			+	3	5				+	1	6
	3	0	7				5	2	4		
+		8	2			+	4	2	5		
		6	1	7	2	5	4	9	1		
	+	2	6	1	4	3	5	0	6		

page 3

	6	7				4	9			3	6
+	2	5			+	2	9		+	3	8
5	6	2				6	5		1	2	2
+	8	3			+	5	3		4	8	5
											1
										6	1
								+	2	1	0
	4	2	7								
+	3	3	5								

©1964 Lore Rasmussen

Ref: *Lab Sheet Annotations*, page 217.

Name____________________ Date____________

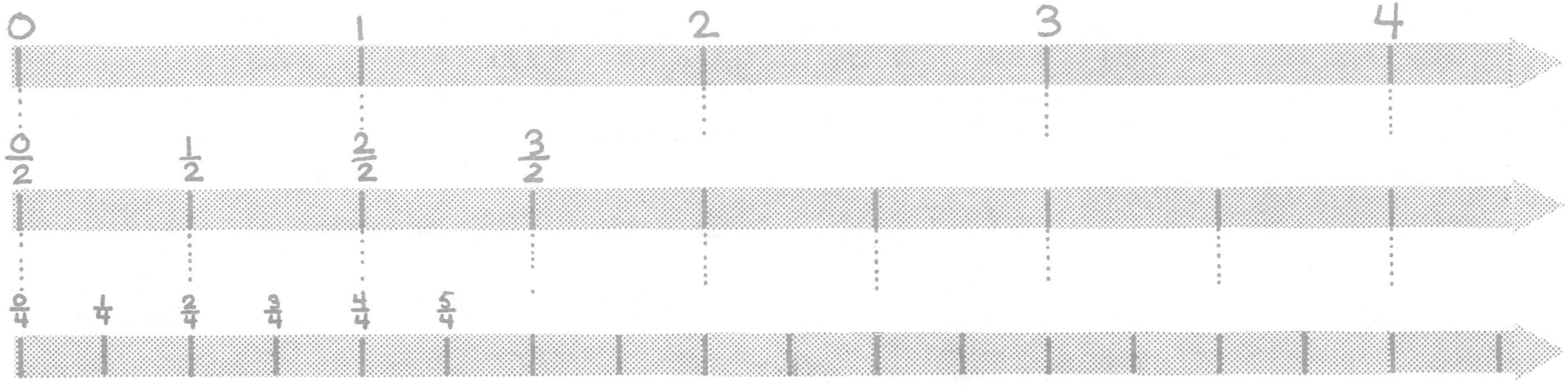

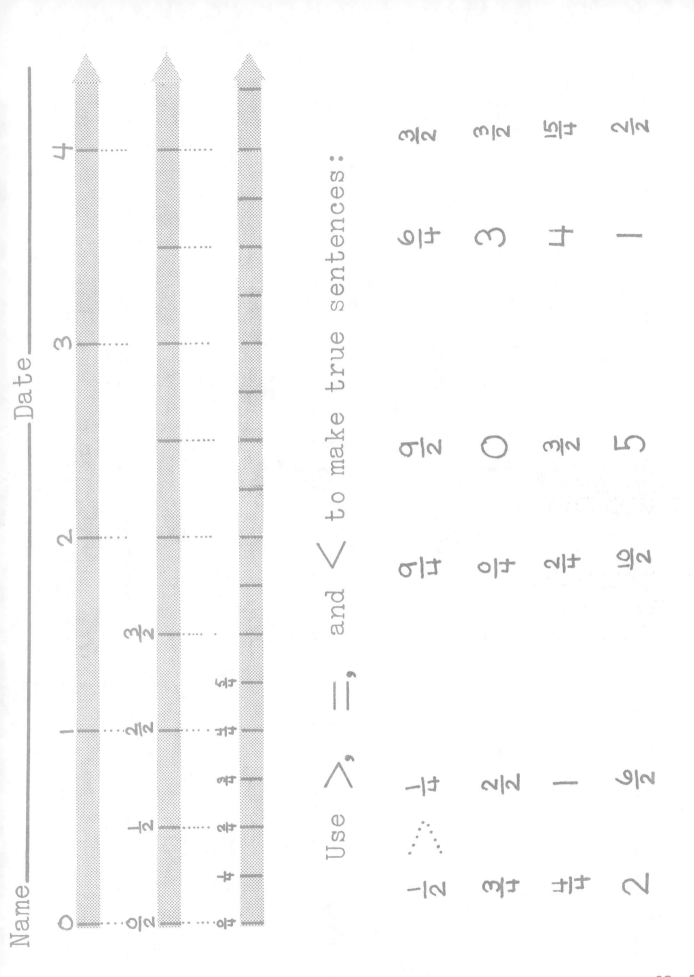

Use >, =, and < to make true sentences:

$\frac{1}{2}$	>	$\frac{1}{4}$	$\frac{9}{4}$	$\frac{9}{2}$	$\frac{6}{4}$	$\frac{3}{2}$
$\frac{3}{4}$		$\frac{2}{2}$	$\frac{0}{4}$	0	3	$\frac{3}{2}$
$\frac{4}{4}$		1	$\frac{2}{4}$	$\frac{3}{2}$	4	$\frac{15}{4}$
2		$\frac{6}{2}$	$\frac{10}{2}$	5	1	$\frac{2}{2}$

©1964 Lore Rasmussen

Ref: *Lab Sheet Annotations*, page 232.

Name ________________________ Date ______________

Label the missing points.

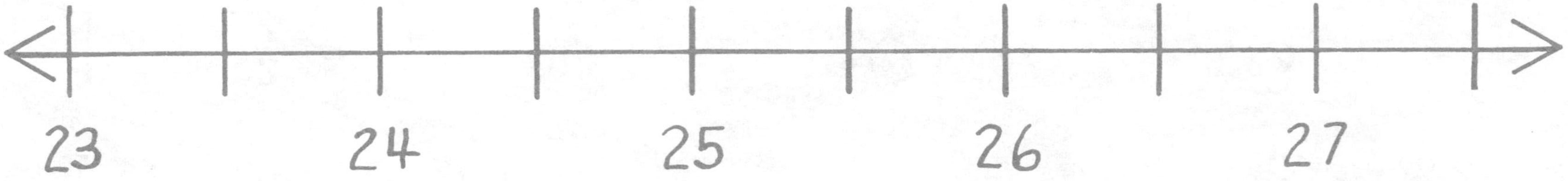

Label the missing points.

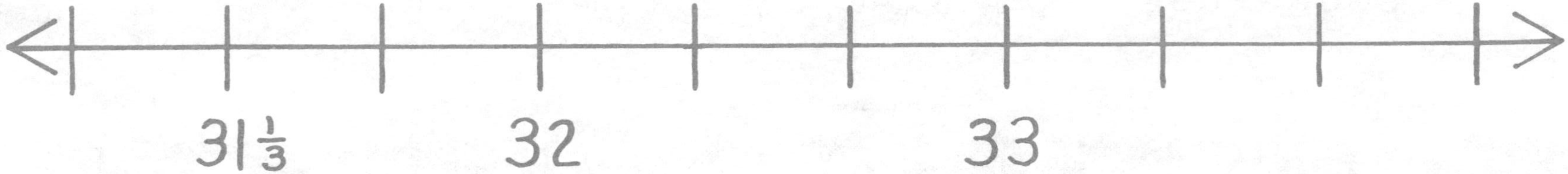

Label the missing points.

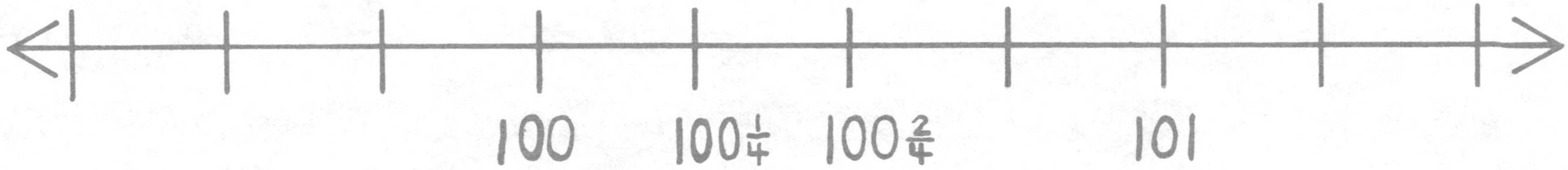

©1964 Lore Rasmussen

Name ______________________ Date ______________

NUMBER LINE GAMES

Billy said, "Play my game. Jump by threes on my number line."

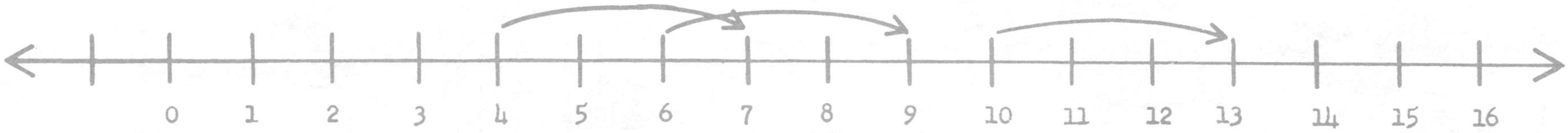

from 4 to 7

from 6 to 9

from 10 to 13

from anywhere to 3 more

□ ⟶ □ + 3

Here is Billy's rule.

□ —Billy⟶ □ +3

4 —B⟶ ○

10 —B⟶ ○

8 —B⟶ ○

12 —B⟶ ○

You try Billy's rule.

0 —B⟶ ○

$\frac{1}{2}$ —B⟶ ○

19 —B⟶ ○

59 —B⟶ ○

22 —B⟶ ○

□ —B⟶ ○

□ —B⟶ ○

□ —B⟶ ○

□ —B⟶ ○

©1964 Lore Rasmussen

Ref: *Lab Sheet Annotations*, page 233.

Name ______________________ Date ______________________

Toni said, "I have a game. Jump on my number line <u>backwards</u> by fours."

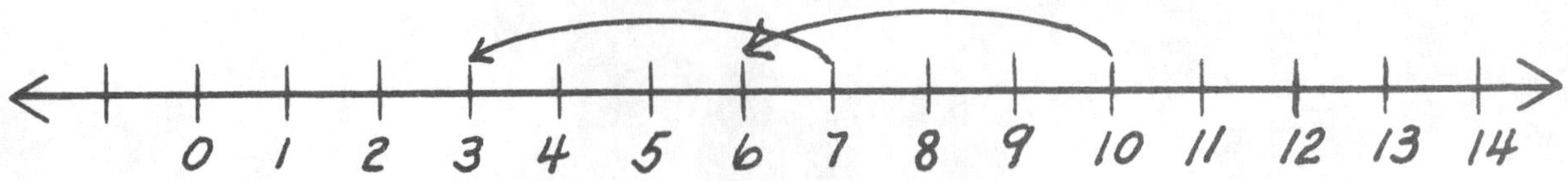

from 7 to 3

from 10 to 6

from anywhere to 4 less

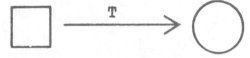

□ → □ - 4

Toni's rule

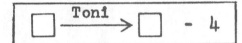

□ —Toni→ □ - 4

7	—T→	◯ (3)
12	—T→	◯
9	—T→	◯
33	—T→	◯
4	—T→	◯
3	—T→	◯
□	—T→	7
□	—T→	52
0	—T→	◯

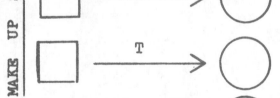

MAKE UP SOME MORE:

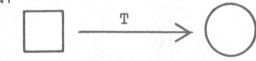

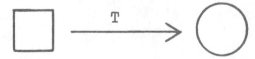

□	—T→	◯
□	—T→	◯
□	—T→	◯
□	—T→	◯
□	—T→	◯
□	—T→	◯
□	—T→	◯
□	—T→	◯
□	—T→	◯
□	—T→	◯

Ref: *Lab Sheet Annotations*, page 233.

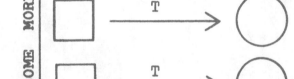

Name ________________________ Date ________________

Ann made a rule. Here it is:

$\square \xrightarrow{A} \square \times 2$

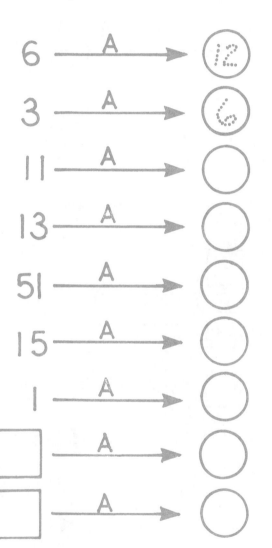

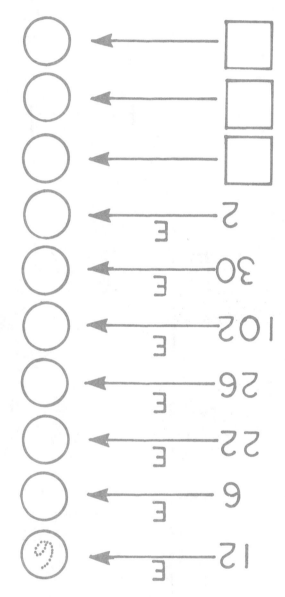

Try Ann's rule:

6 —A→ ◯ (12)

3 —A→ ◯ (6)

11 —A→ ◯

13 —A→ ◯

51 —A→ ◯

15 —A→ ◯

1 —A→ ◯

□ —A→ ◯

□ —A→ ◯

Eddie said, "I have a rule too."

$\square \xrightarrow{E} \frac{1}{2} \times \square$

Now you use Eddie's rule:

12 —E→ ◯ (6)

6 —E→ ◯

22 —E→ ◯

26 —E→ ◯

102 —E→ ◯

30 —E→ ◯

2 —E→ ◯

□ → ◯

□ → ◯

□ → ◯

©1964 Lore Rasmussen

Ref: *Lab Sheet Annotations*, page 235.

Name ______________________ Date ______________________

Make up a number line rule with your name.

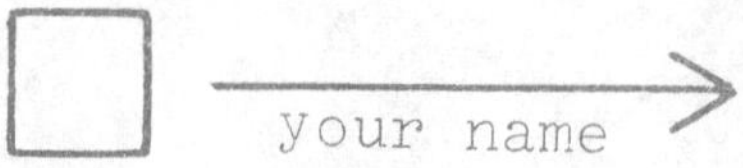

Label the number line.

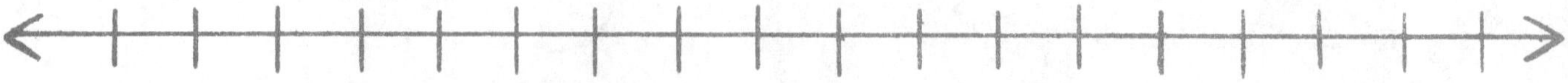

Now make up some jumps using your rule.

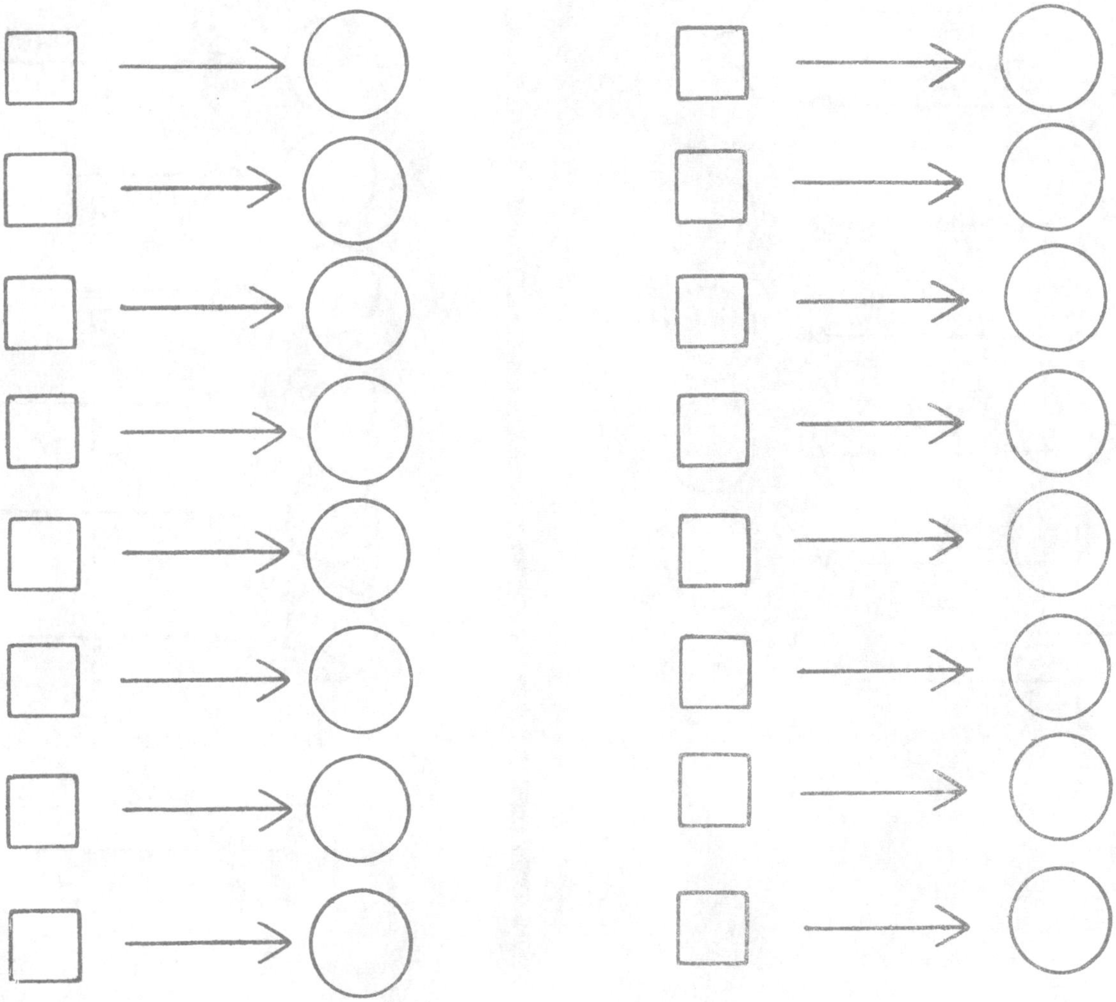

©1978 Lore Rasmussen

Ref: *Lab Sheet Annotations*, page 235.

Name ____________________ Date ____________

Factor House Game

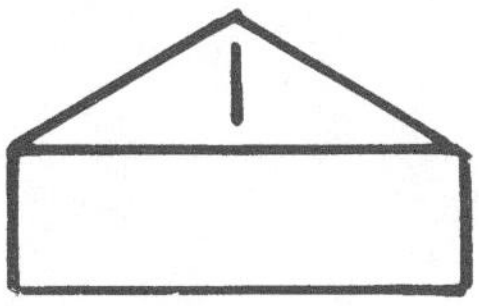

Fill the factor houses.
Then, ask your teacher
how to play this game.
The rules are on the
back of this page.

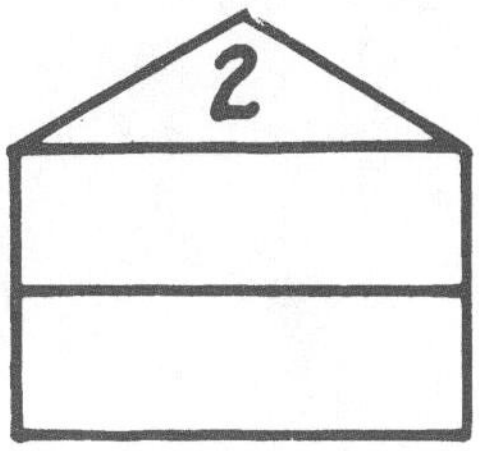

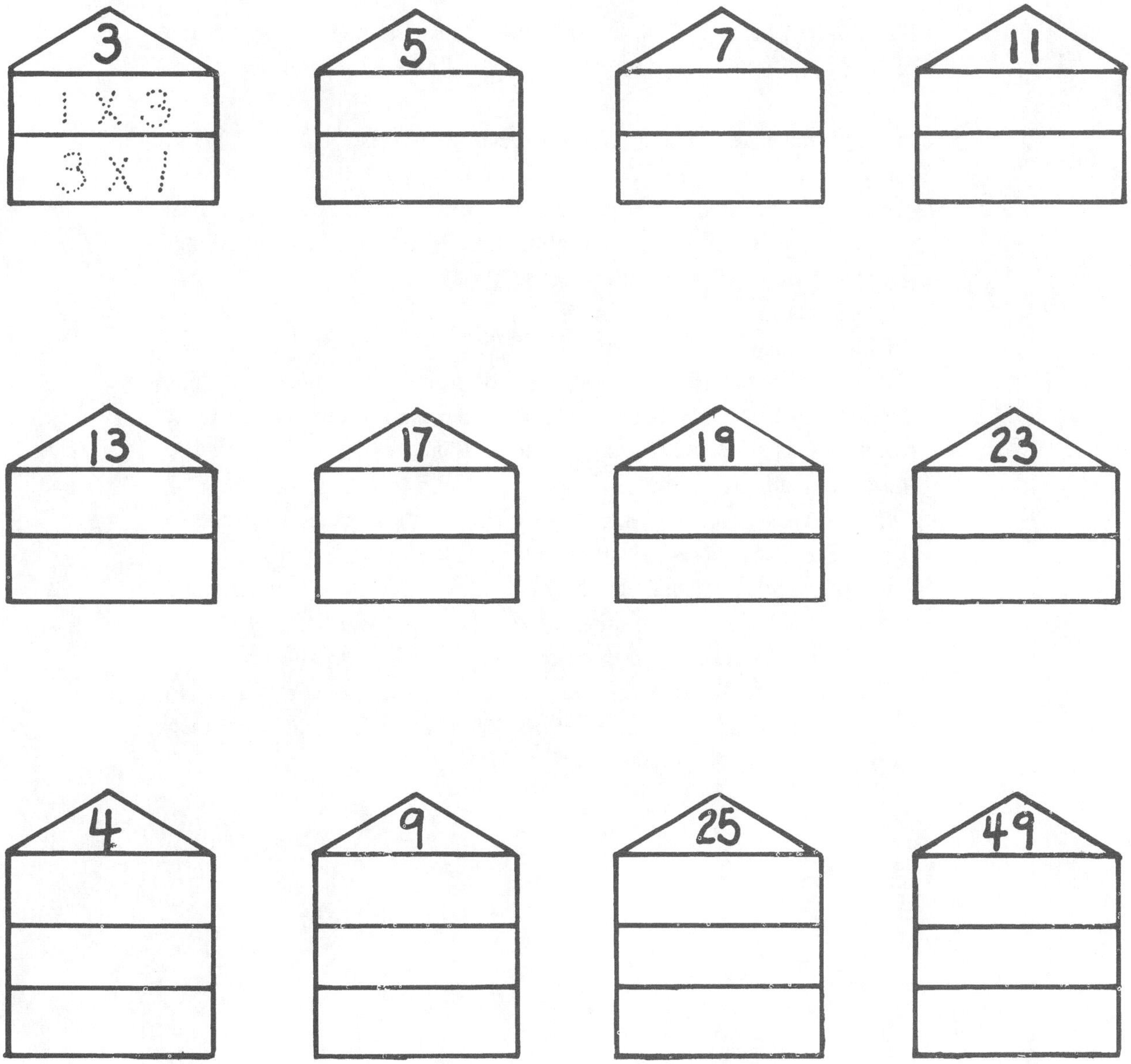

©1964 Lore Rasmussen

Ref: *Lab Sheet Annotations*, page 243.

How to play the House Game

1 Children begin by finding all the ordered pairs of factors of a number. Each pair of factors must be listed on a "floor" of the house.

2 The children cut out their houses and write their own names on the back of each house. Each set of houses should be kept in an envelope.

3 The children take partners and one becomes a seller (Child A) and one a buyer (Child B).

Child A places all the houses from one envelope *face down,* before him on a table. Child B tries to buy the houses from Child A by saying, "I want to buy a ______ story house."

Child A asks, "Who lives in it?"

Child B answers, "Number ______."

If B names the right combination of house and number, B has "bought" the house and takes it. He may then ask for another one from A's pile. This procedure continues until B has either bought all the houses or made an error.

If B makes a mistake, Child A must show him his error and read to him all the "factor families" who live in that number's house.

Child A may call "Challenge!" if B is *very* good. Then B must name all the families for that number before he gets the house. No seller may ever ask for more than three challenges during any one game.

The game ends when B has all the houses or makes a mistake. He writes down his score (one point for each house bought) and then takes his place as the seller.

Name______________________ Date________________

Factor Houses

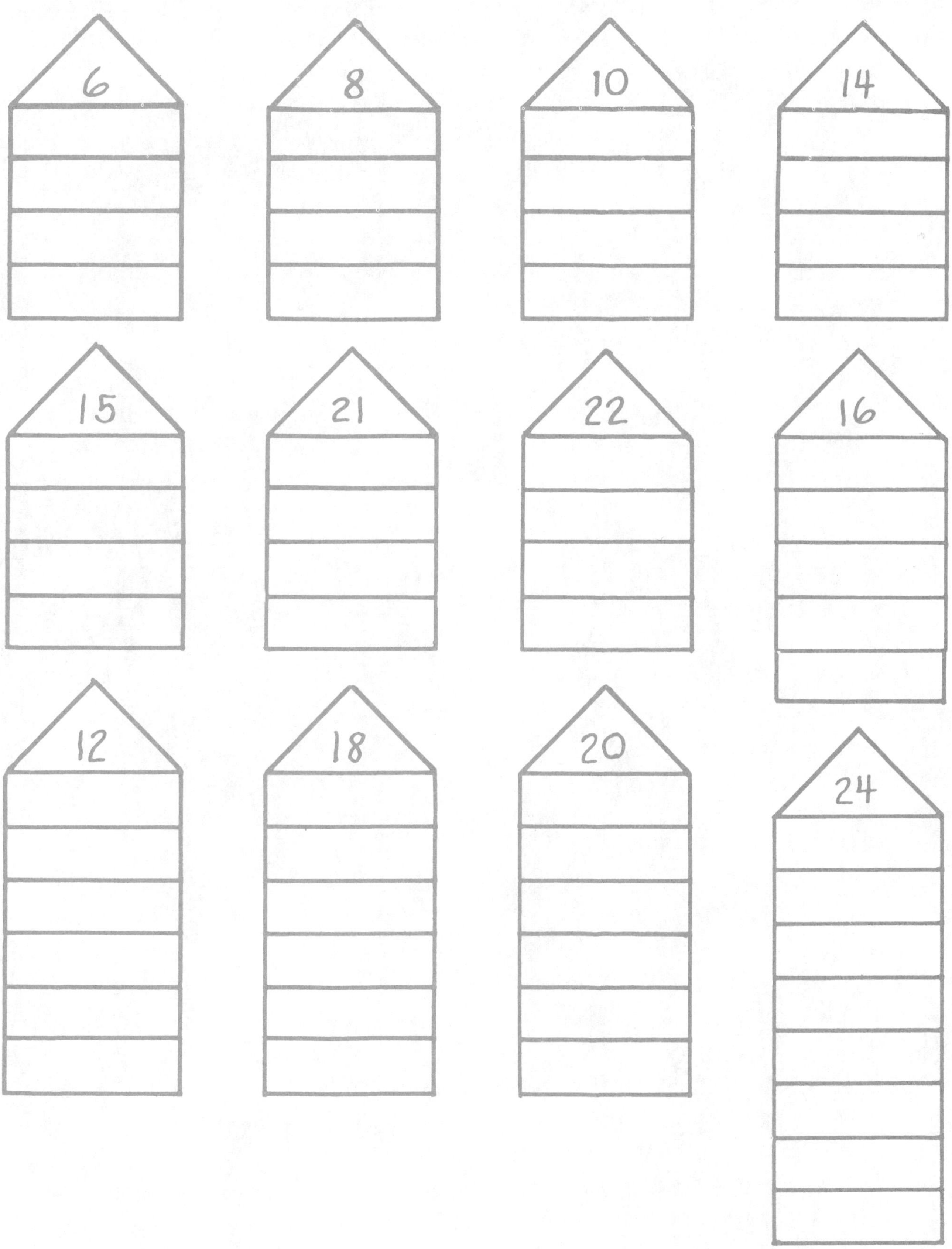

©1964 Lore Rasmussen

Ref: *Lab Sheet Annotations,* page 243.

Name ______________________ Date ______________

1	2	3		5
6		8		
11			14	
16	17			20
		23		

1		
4	5	6
	8	

	2	3	
5	6		8
		11	
13	14		16

Square Numbers

1	2
	4

1			4	5	
7	8			11	12
	14	15		17	
19			22		24
25	26	27	28		
31		33		35	36

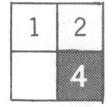

©1964 Lore Rasmussen

Ref: *Lab Sheet Annotations*, page 248.

Name ______________________

Date ______________________

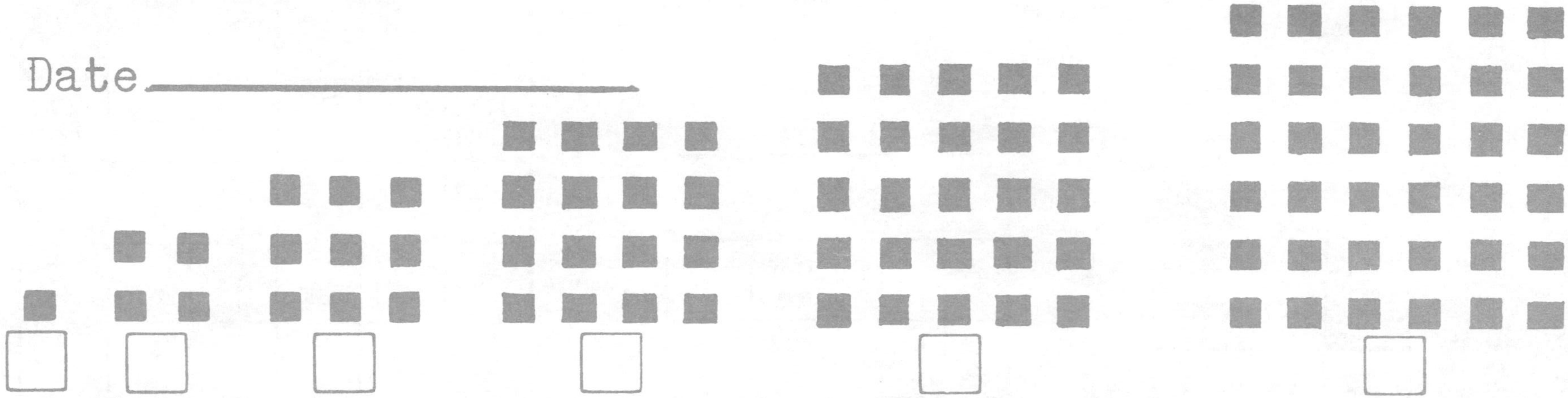

Square Numbers

©1964 Lore Rasmussen

Ref: *Lab Sheet Annotations,* page 248.

Name ______________________ Date ______________

← 1 sq. inch

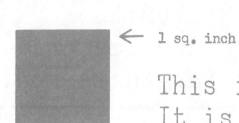

This is the square unit.
It is one square inch.

_____ square unit will cover this square.

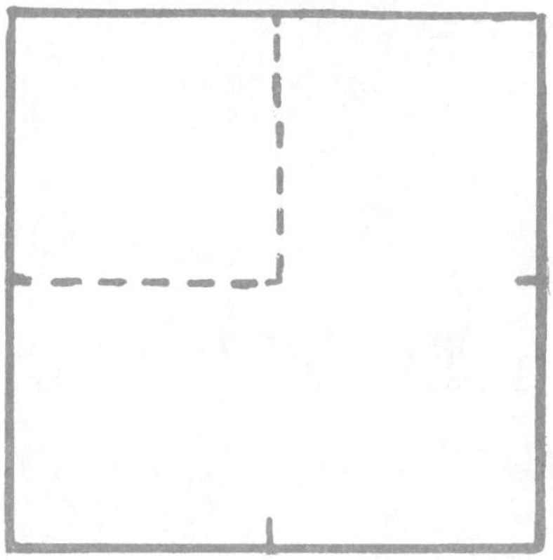

_____ square units will cover this square.

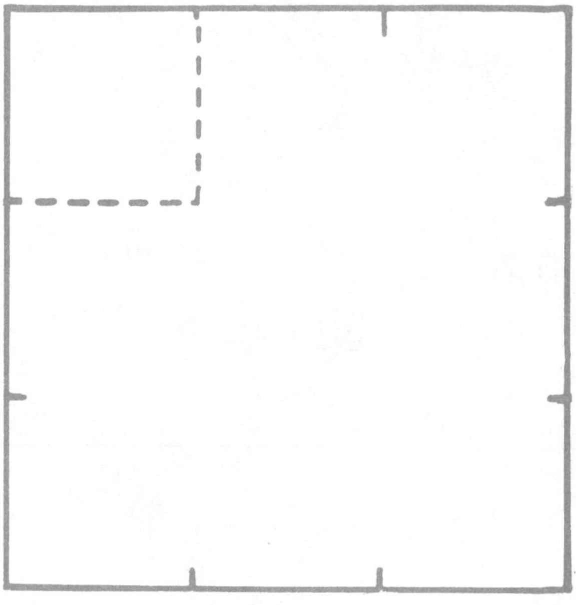

_____ square units will cover this square.

©1964 Lore Rasmussen

Ref: *Lab Sheet Annotations*, page 248.

Name ______________________ Date ____________

1 sq. centimeter

 ← This is the square unit.
It is one square centimeter.
It is the same size as the white rod.

_____ square unit will cover this square.

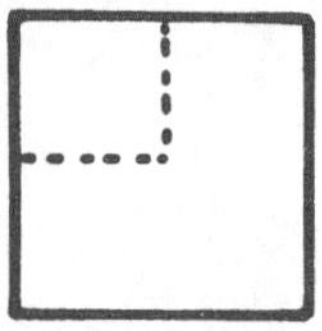

_____ square units will cover this square.

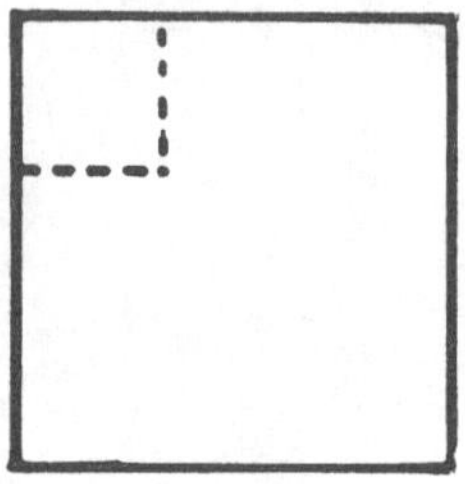

_____ square units will cover this square.

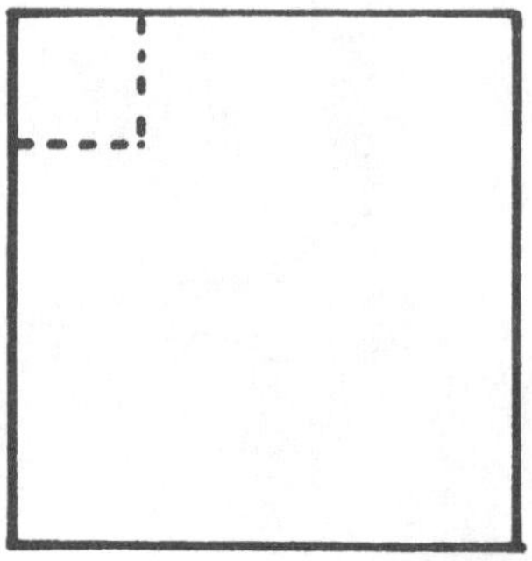

_____ square units will cover this square.

©1964 Lore Rasmussen

Ref: *Lab Sheet Annotations*, page 248.

Name ______________________ Date ________________

Cover each picture with rods.

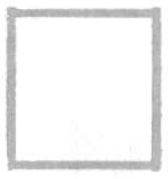

1 X 1 =

2 X 2 =

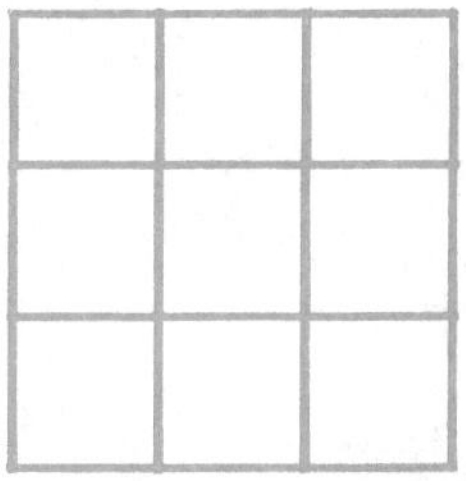

3 X 3 =

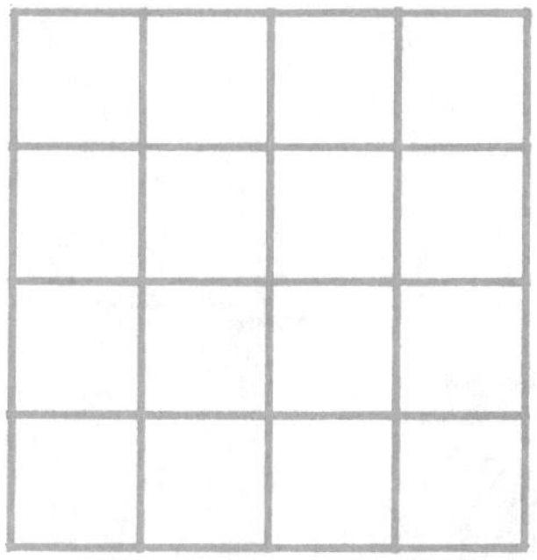

4 X 4 =

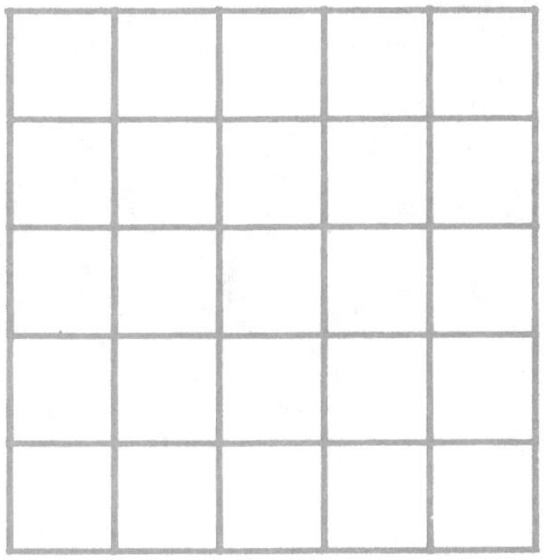

5 X 5 =

©1964 Lore Rasmussen

Ref: *Lab Sheet Annotations*, page 248.

Name ______________________ Date ______________________

COVER WITH RODS

1^2 ⬡ x ⬡ $= 1^2$

2^2 ⬡ x ⬡ $= 2^2$

3^2 ⬡ x ⬡ $= 3^2$

4^2 ⬡ x ⬡ $= 4^2$

5^2 ⬡ x ⬡ $= 5^2$

©1964 Lore Rasmussen

Name ______________________________ Date ____________________

$1^2 = 1 \times 1 = \square$

$2^2 = 2 \times 2 = \square$

$3^2 = 3 \times 3 = \square$

$4^2 = 4 \times 4 = \square$

$5^2 = 5 \times 5 = \square$

$6^2 = 6 \times 6 = \square$

$7^2 = 7 \times 7 = \square$

$8^2 = 8 \times 8 = \square$

$9^2 = 9 \times 9 = \square$

$10^2 = 10 \times 10 = \square$

Use Rods When You Need Help

©1964 Lore Rasmussen

Ref: *Lab Sheet Annotations*, page 250.

Name________________________ Date________________

Find the missing square numbers.
Shade them into the chart.

$1^2 =$ [ ]

$2^2 =$ [ ] $5^2 =$ [ ] $8^2 =$ [ ]

$3^2 =$ [ ] $6^2 =$ [ ] $9^2 =$ [ ]

$4^2 =$ [16] $7^2 =$ [49] $10^2 =$ [100]

1	2	3	4	5	6	7	8	9	10
11	12	13	14	15	16	17	18	19	20
21	22	23	24	25	26	27	28	29	30
31	32	33	34	35	36	37	38	39	40
41	42	43	44	45	46	47	48	49	50
51	52	53	54	55	56	57	58	59	60
61	62	63	64	65	66	67	68	69	70
71	72	73	74	75	76	77	78	79	80
81	82	83	84	85	86	87	88	89	90
91	92	93	94	95	96	97	98	99	100

©1964 Lore Rasmussen

Name ______________________ Date ______________________

Draw a line connecting names for the same number.

1^2	4
2^2	25
3^2	36
4^2	81
5^2	9
6^2	100
7^2	64
8^2	49
9^2	1
10^2	16

©1964 Lore Rasmussen

Ref: *Lab Sheet Annotations*, page 251.

Name ______________________ Date ______________________

Draw a line connecting two names for the same number.

36	5^2
41	7^2
25	3^2
90	6^2
8	2^2
4	4^2
16	8^2
81	10^2
54	9^2
49	
9	
100	

©1964 Lore Rasmussen

Ref: *Lab Sheet Annotations*, page 251.

Name________________________________ Date ______________

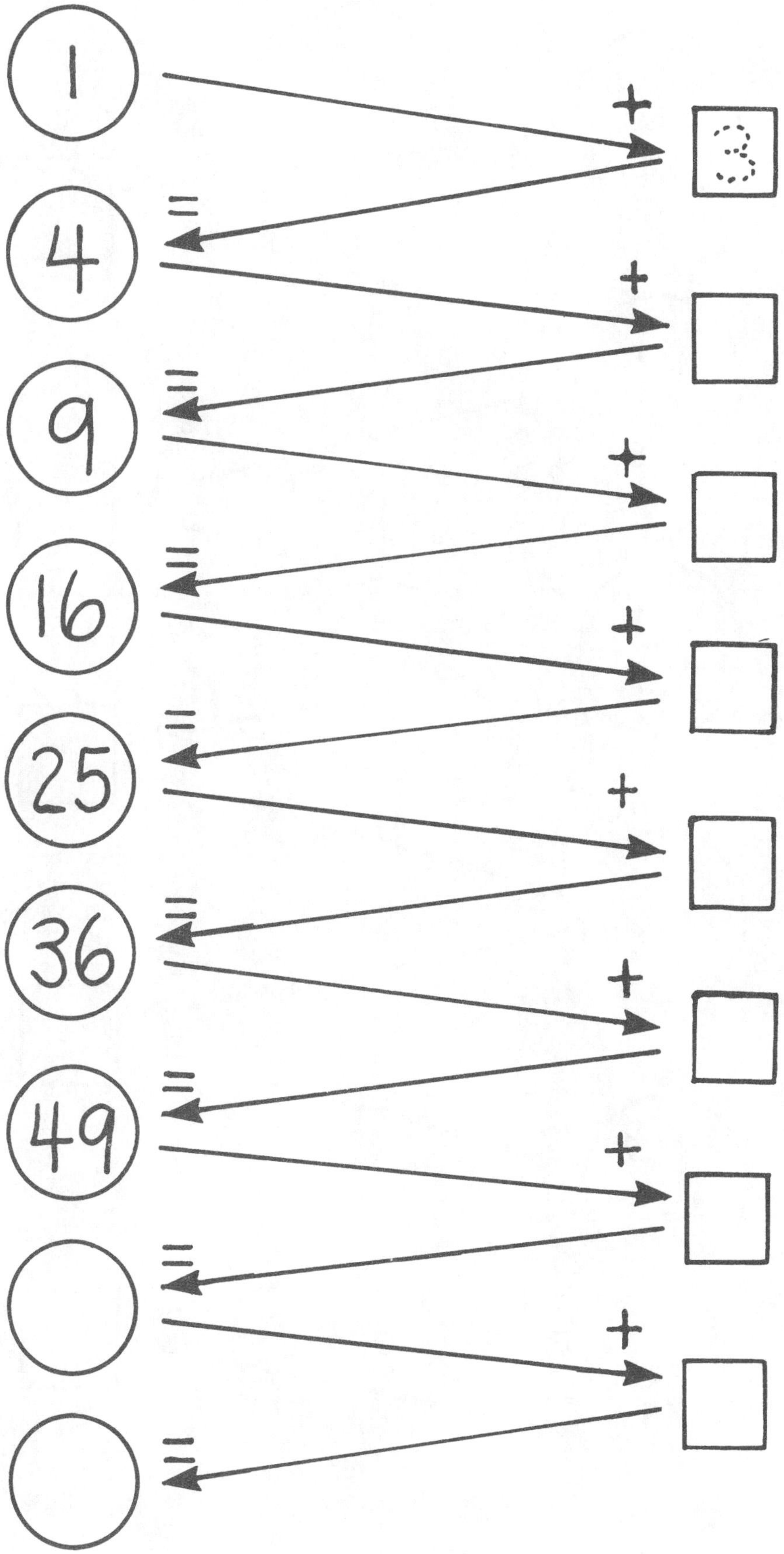

©1964 Lore Rasmussen

Ref: *Lab Sheet Annotations*, page 252.

Name ______________________________ Date ____________________

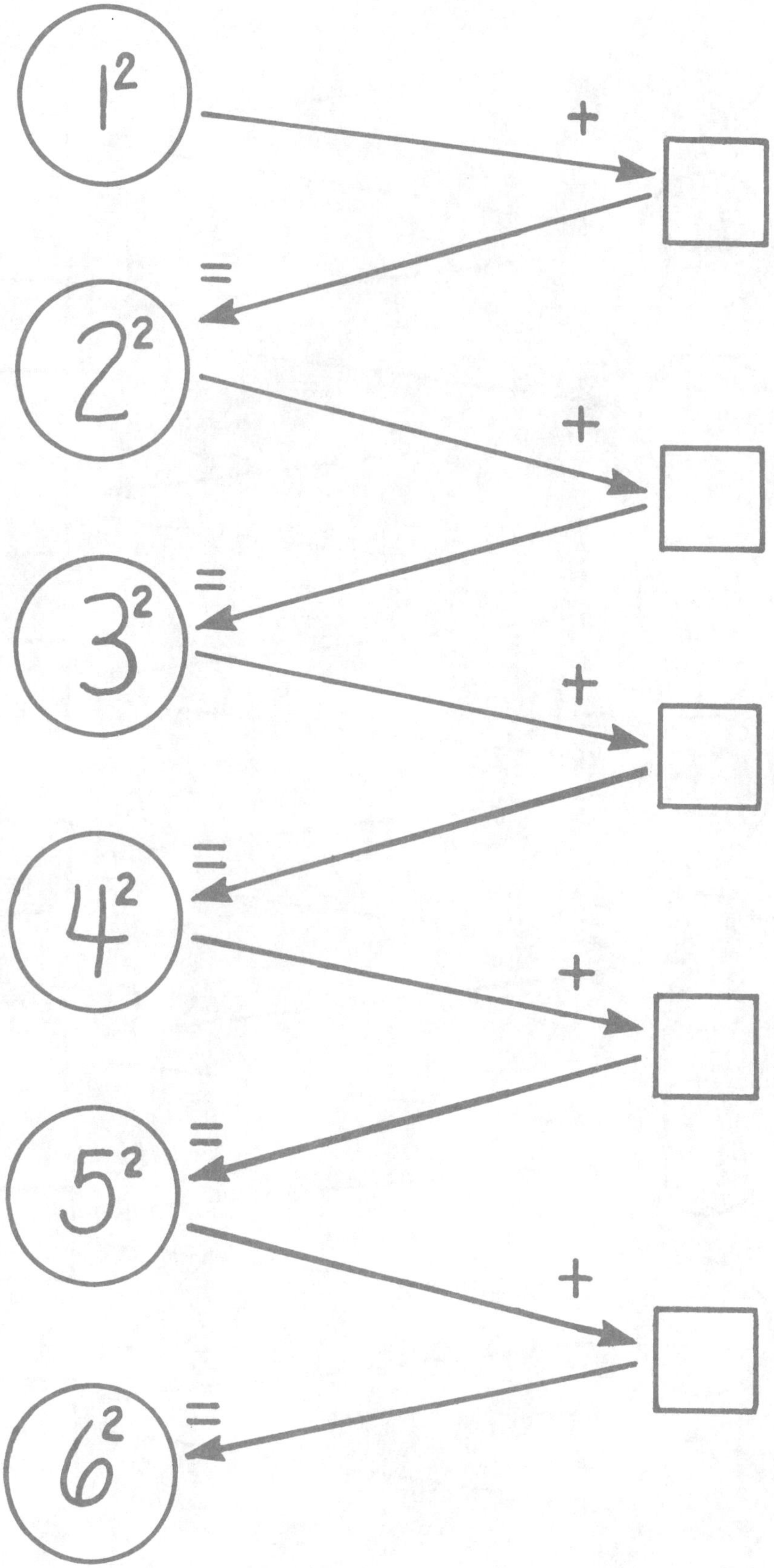

©1964 Lore Rasmussen

Ref: *Lab Sheet Annotations*, page 252.

Name ______________________________ Date ____________________

$4 = 2 \times \square$

$5 \times \square = 25$

$\square \times 3 = 9$

$1 \times \square = 1$

$10 \times 10 = \square$

$6 \times \square = 36$

$5^2 = \square \times \square$

$9^2 = \bigcirc \times \bigcirc$

$36{,}921^2 = \square \times \square$

$999^2 = \square \times \square$

©1964 Lore Rasmussen

Name ______________________ Date ______________________

Read the problems and divide the dots. Write the answers in the boxes.

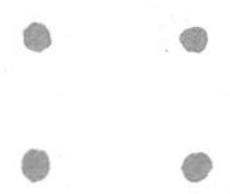

How many 2's in 4?

$4 \div 2 = \square$

Five of what number equals 25?

$25 \div \square = 5$

How many 3's in 9?

$9 \div 3 = \square$

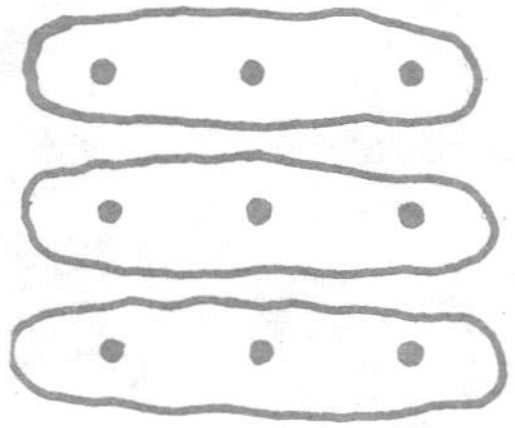

How many dots have been divided?

$\square \div 3 = 3$

How many 4's in 16?

$16 \div 4 = \square$

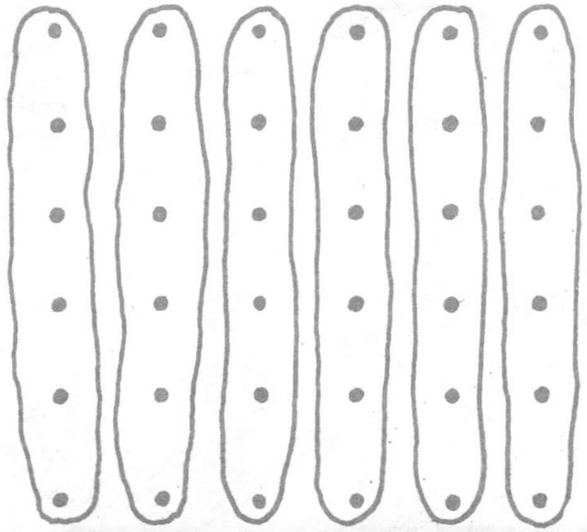

How many dots have been divided?

$\square \div 6 = 6$

©1964 Lore Rasmussen

Ref: *Lab Sheet Annotations*, page 253.

Name ____________________ Date ____________

$4 \div 2 = \square$

$9 \div 3 = \square$

$16 \div 4 = \square$

$25 \div 5 = \square$

$36 \div 6 = \square$

$49 \div 7 = \square$

$64 \div 8 = \square$

$81 \div 9 = \square$

$100 \div 10 = \square$

$\square \div 3 = 3$

$\square \div 4 = 4$

$\square \div 5 = 5$

©1964 Lore Rasmussen

Ref: *Lab Sheet Annotations*, page 253.

Name ______________________ Date ______________________

$$1 \times 1 = 0 \times 0 + \square$$
$$2 \times 2 = 1 \times 1 + \square$$
$$3 \times 3 = 2 \times 2 + \square$$
$$4 \times 4 = 3 \times 3 + \square$$
$$5 \times 5 = 4 \times 4 + \square$$
$$6 \times 6 = 5 \times 5 + \square$$
$$7 \times 7 = 6 \times 6 + \square$$
$$8 \times 8 = 7 \times 7 + \square$$
$$9 \times 9 = 8 \times 8 + \square$$
$$10 \times 10 = 9 \times 9 + \square$$

$$2^2 - 1^2 = 2 + \square$$
$$3^2 - 2^2 = 3 + \square$$
$$4^2 - 3^2 = 4 + \square$$
$$5^2 - 4^2 = \bigcirc + \square$$
$$6^2 - 5^2 = \bigcirc + \square$$

©1964 Lore Rasmussen
Ref: *Lab Sheet Annotations*, page 254.

Name______________________________ Date______________________

Make a train ten orange rods long.

Your train is one meter long.

Look at your one meter long train when you do lab sheet ....T-8b.

©1978 Lore Rasmussen

Name ______________________ Date ______________

Estimate.

	MUCH SHORTER THAN ONE METER	SHORTER THAN ONE METER	ABOUT ONE METER	LONGER THAN ONE METER	MUCH LONGER THAN ONE METER
My finger is ...	✓				
I am ...					
A pencil is ...					
A telephone pole is...					
My teacher is ...					
My arm is ...					
My bed is ...					
A fly is ...					
A bus is ...					
A baseball bat is ...					

©1978 Lore Rasmussen

100　centimeters　=　1　meter

200　centimeters　=　☐　meters

300　centimeters　=　☐　meters

400　centimeters　=　☐　meters

500　centimeters　=　☐　meters

☐　centimeters　=　6　meters

☐　centimeters　=　7　meters

800　centimeters　=　☐　meters

900　centimeters　=　☐　meters

☐　centimeters　=　10　meters

cm ←→ centimeters	m ←→ meters

123　cm　=　1　m　+　23　cm

150　cm　=　◯　m　+　50　cm

245　cm　=　2　m　+　⬡　cm

321　cm　=　◯　m　+　⬡　cm

☐　cm　=　4　m　+　83　cm

©1978 Lore Rasmussen

Name ____________________ Date __________

>, =, or <

1 cm ○ 1 m

150 cm ○ 1 m + 50 cm

1 m ○ 72 cm

125 cm ○ 2 m

6 m ○ 6 cm

100 cm ○ 1 m

100 m ○ 1 cm

146 cm ○ 1 m + 40 cm

3 m ○ 300 cm

2 m + 50 cm ○ 3 m

©1978 Lore Rasmussen

Name____________________ Date______________

Cover with rods.

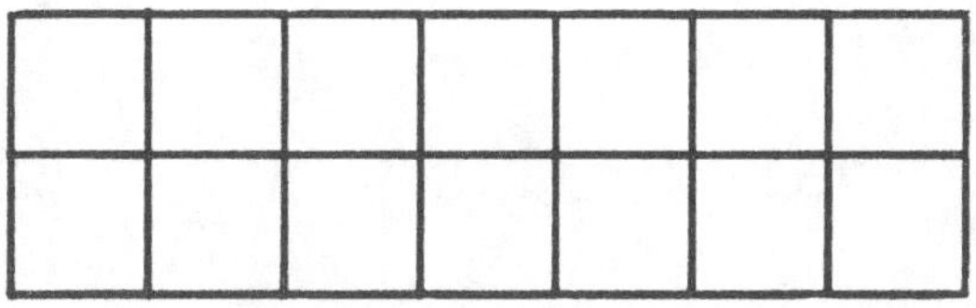

14 square centimeters

cover the inside.

The area is 14 cm^2.

Cover with rods.

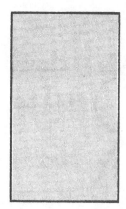

_____ cm^2 cover the inside. The area is _____ cm^2.

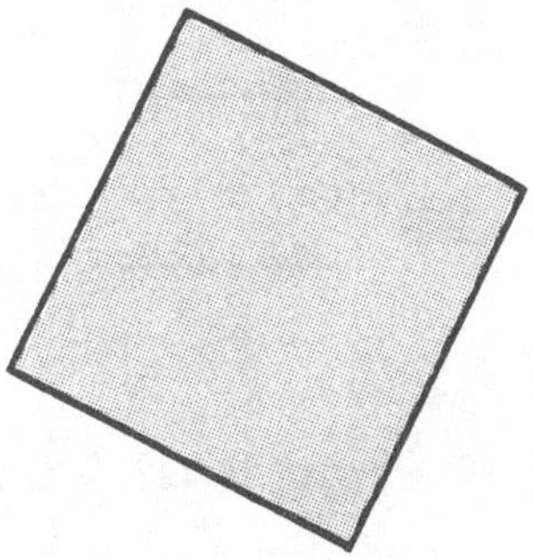

The area is _____ cm^2.

The line around the outside is _____ cm.

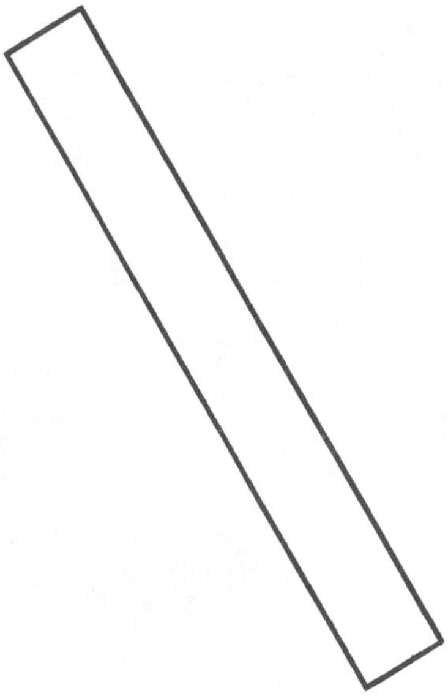

The line around the outside is _____ cm.

The area is _____ cm^2.

Get rods, paper and pencil and make some more papers like this.

©1978 Lore Rasmussen

Ref: *Lab Sheet Annotations*, page 296.

Name ______________________ Date ______________________

This rectangle is _____ cm long.

This rectangle is _____ cm wide.

white rods will fill the rectangle.

red rods will fill the rectangle.

This rectangle is _____ cm long.

This rectangle is _____ cm wide.

white rods will fill the rectangle.

red rods will fill the rectangle.

green rods will fill the rectangle.

This rectangle is _____ cm long.

This rectangle is _____ cm wide.

white rods will fill the rectangle.

red rods will fill the rectangle.

green rods will fill the rectangle.

©1964 Lore Rasmussen

Ref: *Lab Sheet Annotations*, page 296.

Name ____________________ Date ____________________

Use rods to find the areas

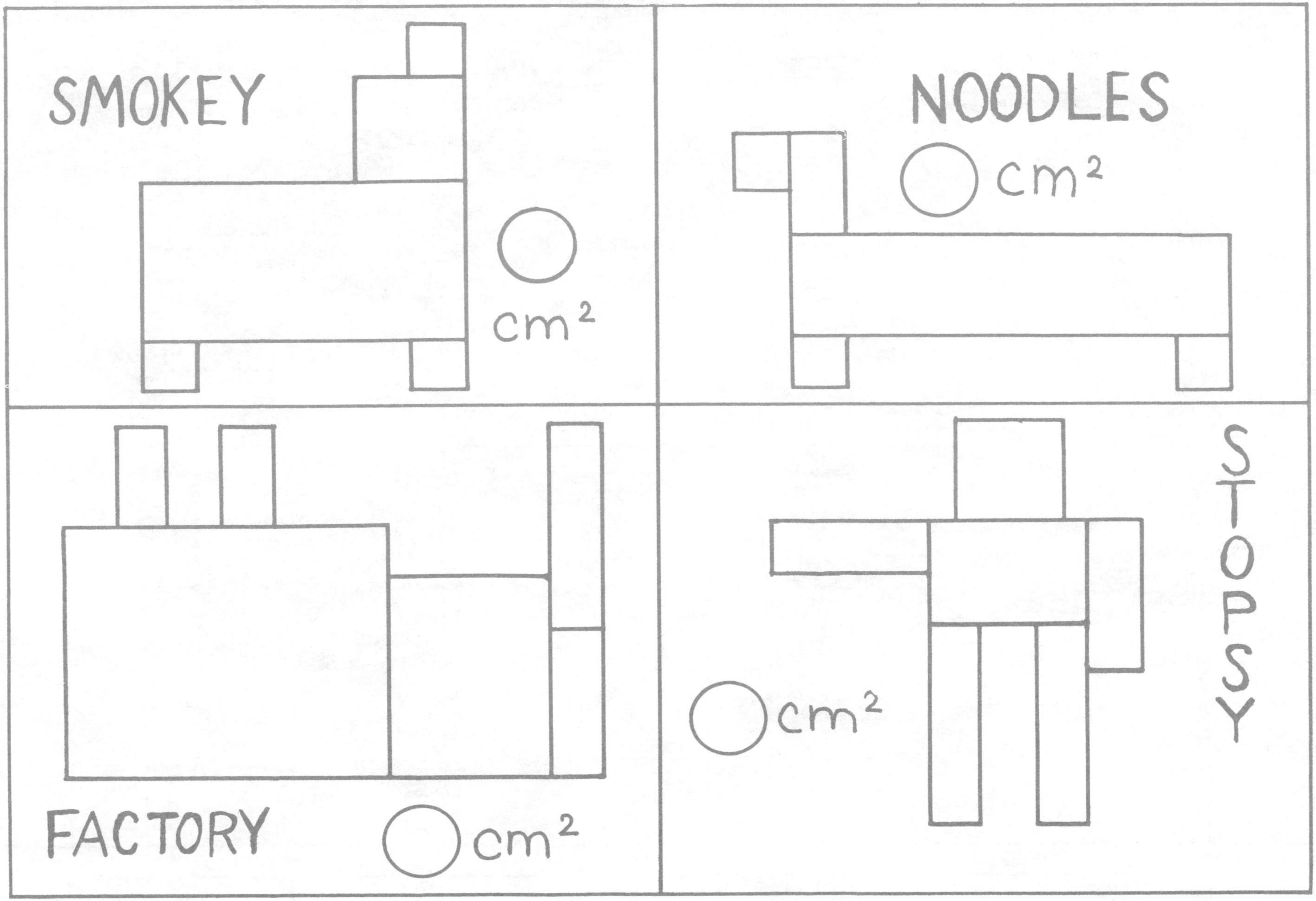

©1964 Lore Rasmussen

Name ______________________ Date ______________

USE RODS OR RULER.

Measure all around Smokey's shadow.
It measures ____________ centimeters.

Measure all around Noodles' shadow.
It measures ____________ centimeters.

Measure all around the factory's shadow.
It measures ____________ centimeters.

The measure all around a figure is called the PERIMETER.

©1964 Lore Rasmussen

Ref: *Lab Sheet Annotations*, page 297.

Name ______________________ Date ______________

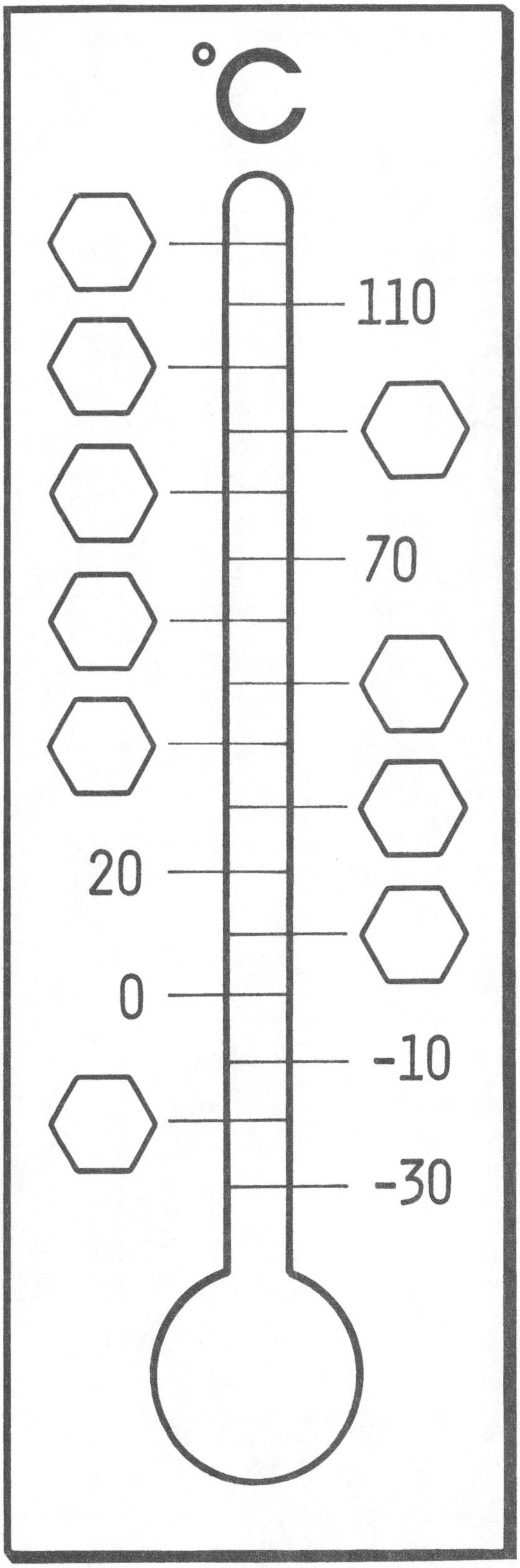

CELSIUS THERMOMETER

©1978 Lore Rasmussen

Name ______________________ Date ______________________

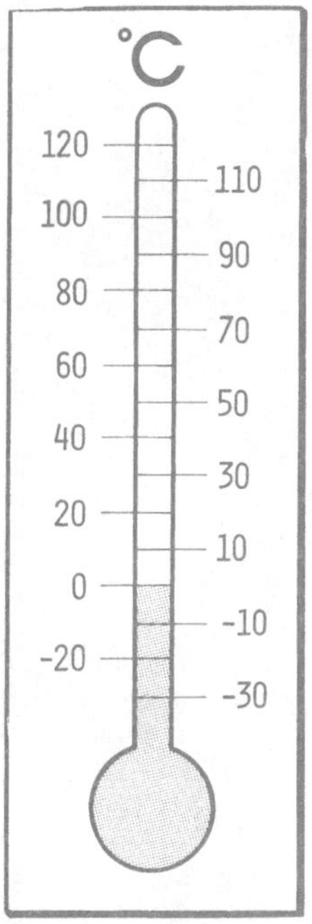

water freezes

This thermometer shows 0 degrees Celsius.

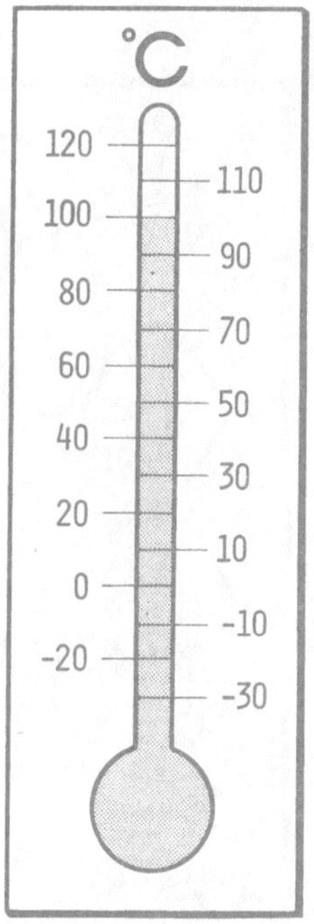

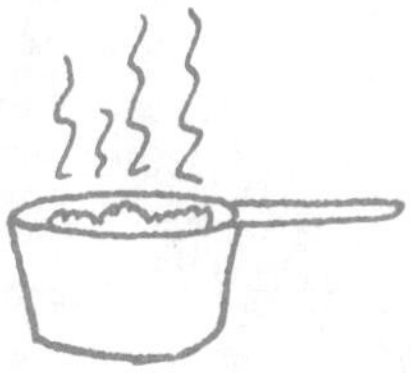

water boils

This thermometer shows 100 degrees Celsius.

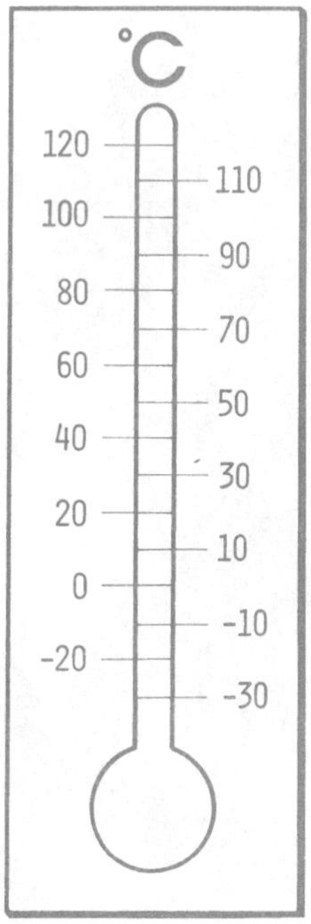

cool day

Color this thermometer to show 10 degrees Celsius.

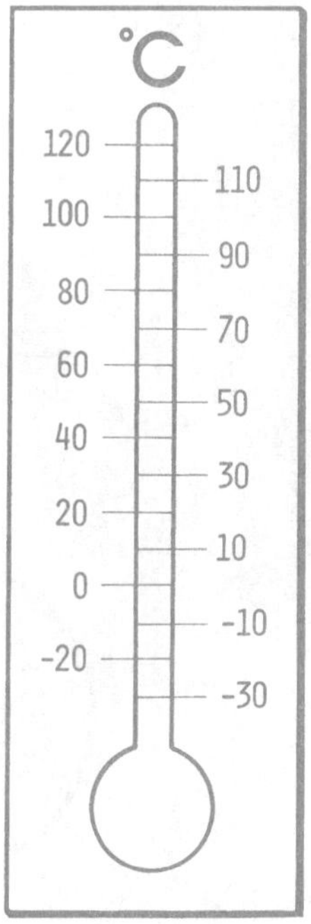

comfortable room temperature

Color this thermometer to show 20 degrees Celsius.

©1978 Lore Rasmussen

Name ______________________ Date ______________

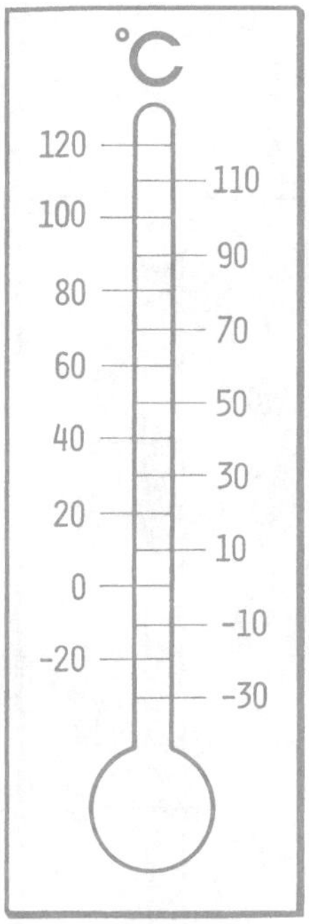

warm
summer
day

Color this thermometer to show 25 degrees Celsius.

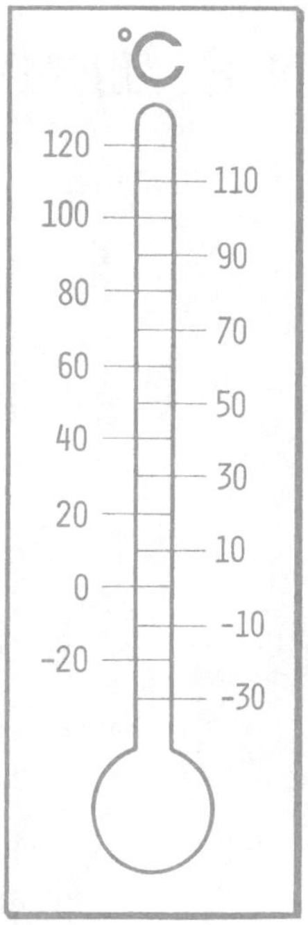

hottest day
ever
recorded

Color this thermometer to show 58 degrees Celsius.

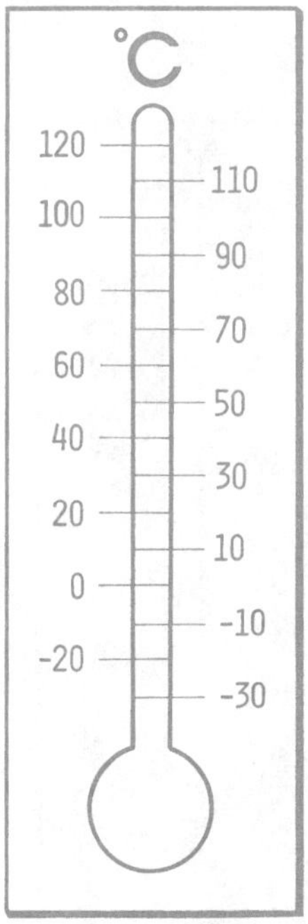

normal
body
temperature

Color this thermometer to show 37 degrees Celsius.

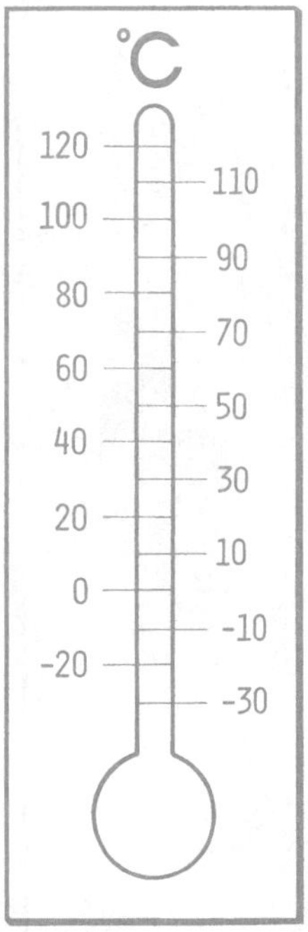

snowy
winter
day

Color this thermometer to show -10 degrees Celsius.

©1978 Lore Rasmussen

Name ______________________________ Date ____________

THE TEMPERATURE IS...

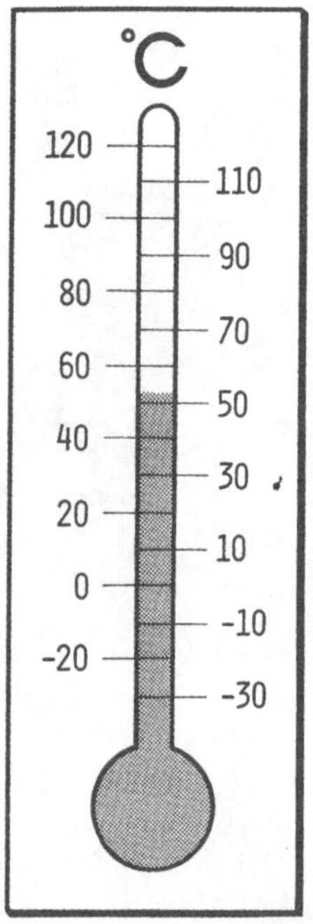

about 52° Celsius

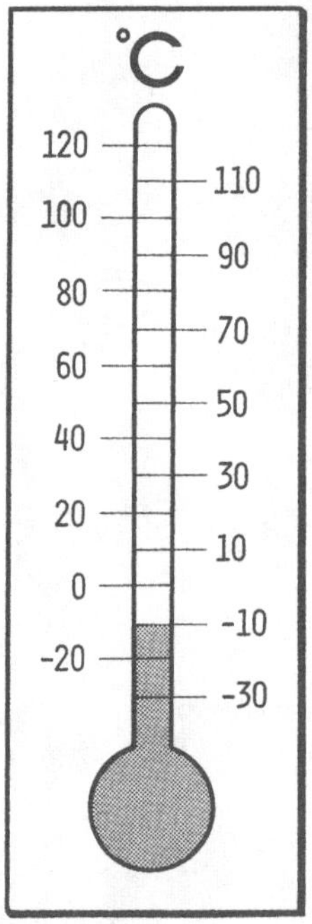

about -10° Celsius

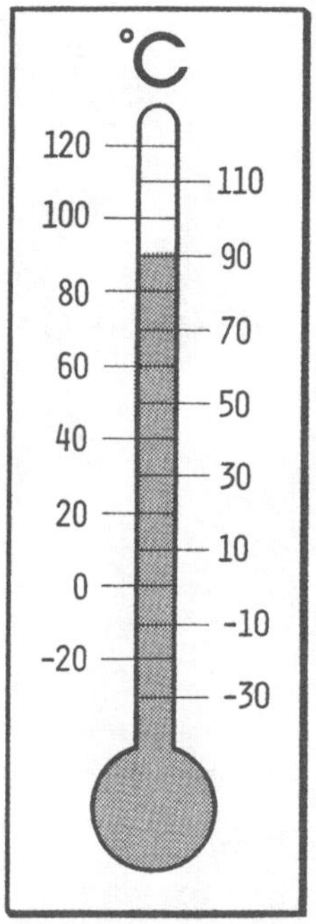

about ______°Celsius

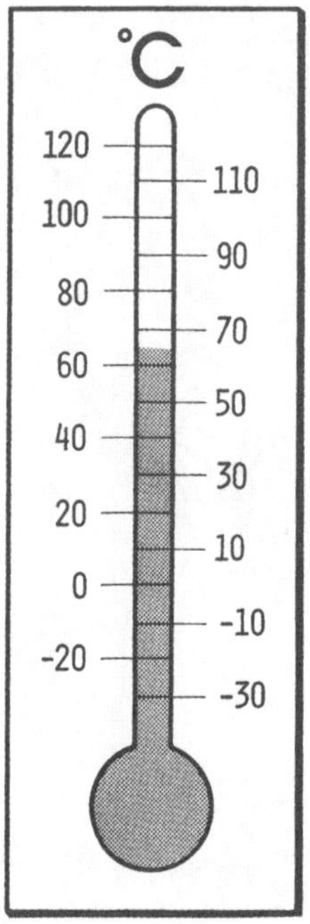

about______° Celsius

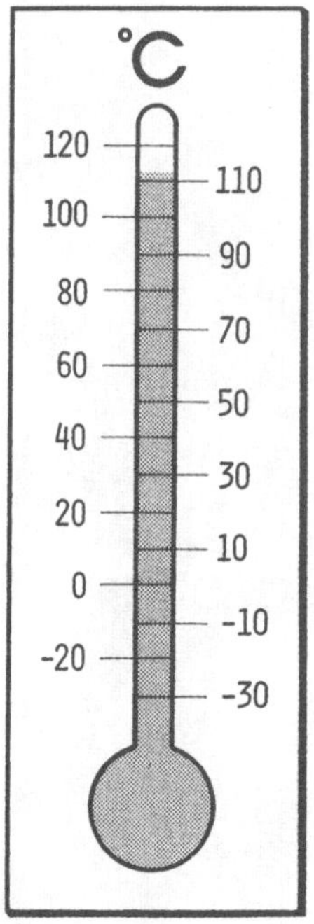

about______° Celsius

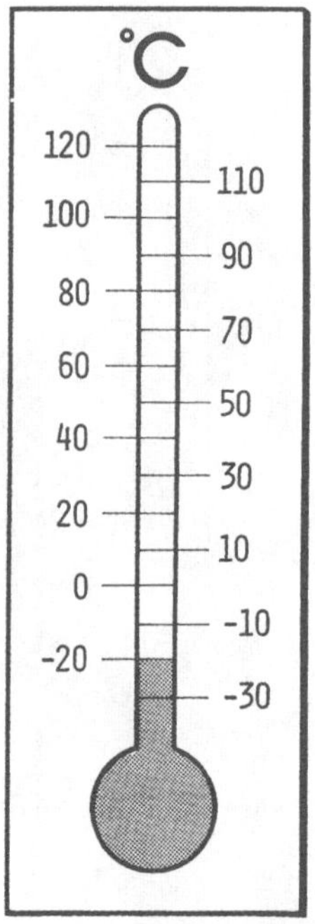

about______° Celsius

©1978 Lore Rasmussen

Name ______________________ Date ______________

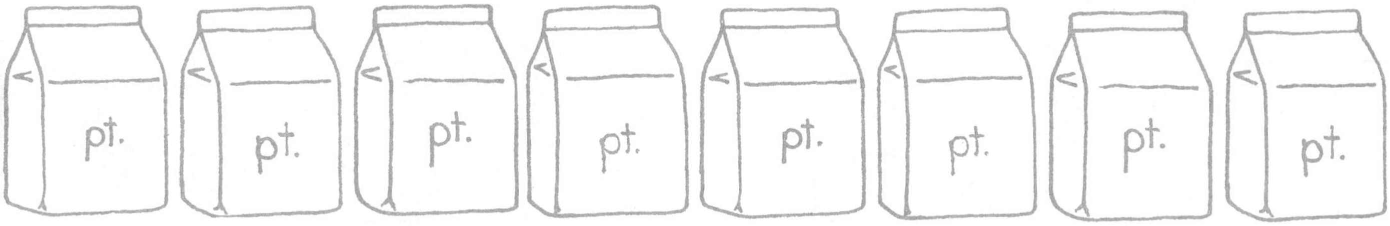

8 pints = 1 gallon

c. ↔ cup
pt. ↔ pint
qt. ↔ quart
gal. ↔ gallon

16 cups = 1 gallon
8 pints = 1 gallon
4 quarts = 1 gallon

4 quarts = 1 gallon

16 cups = 1 gallon

©1978 Lore Rasmussen

Ref: *Lab Sheet Annotations*, page 299.

Name ______________________ Date ______________________

Cross out any extra cups.

Cross out any extra cups.

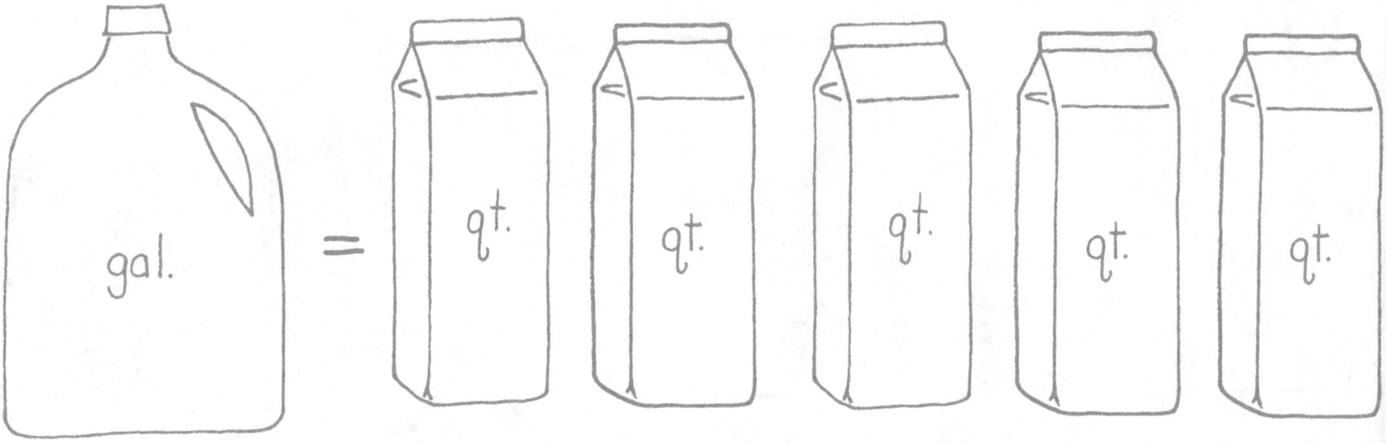

Cross out any extra quarts.

6 cups = ☐ pints

12 cups = ☐ quarts

2 quarts = ☐ cups

☐ pints = 1 gallon

2 gallons = ☐ quarts

©1978 Lore Rasmussen

Ref: *Lab Sheet Annotations*, page 299.

Name ____________________ Date ______________

Use your rods.

If the white rod stands for one cup, then:

one cup

one pint

one quart

one gallon

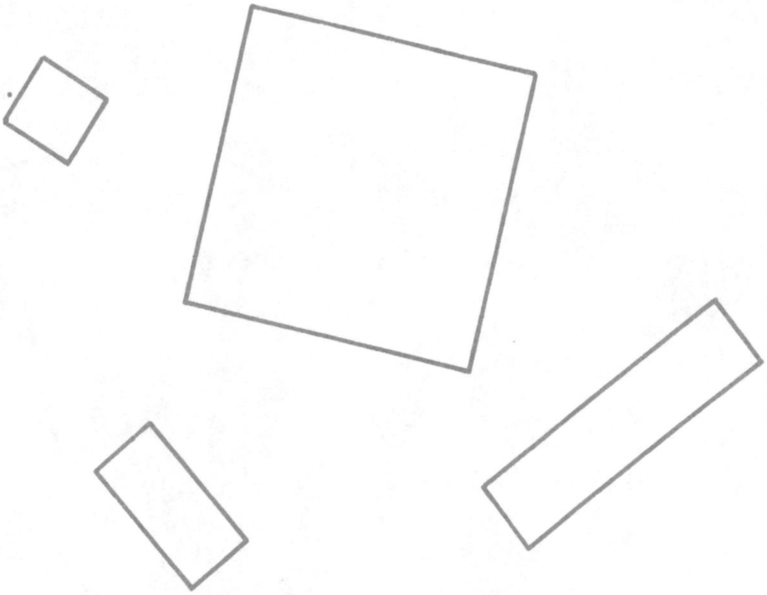

one gallon = ___ quarts = ___ pints = ___ cups

one quart = ___ gallon = ___ pints = ___ cups

one pint = ___ gallon = ___ quart = ___ cups

one cup = ___ gallon = ___ quart = ___ pint

©1964 Lore Rasmussen

Ref: *Lab Sheet Annotations*, page 299.

Name____________________ Date________________

Draw a line from rod to measure.

Let ☐ stand for <u>one</u> <u>cup</u>.

THEN

2 pints

3 cups

1 quart

4 cups

$1\frac{1}{2}$ pints

2 cups

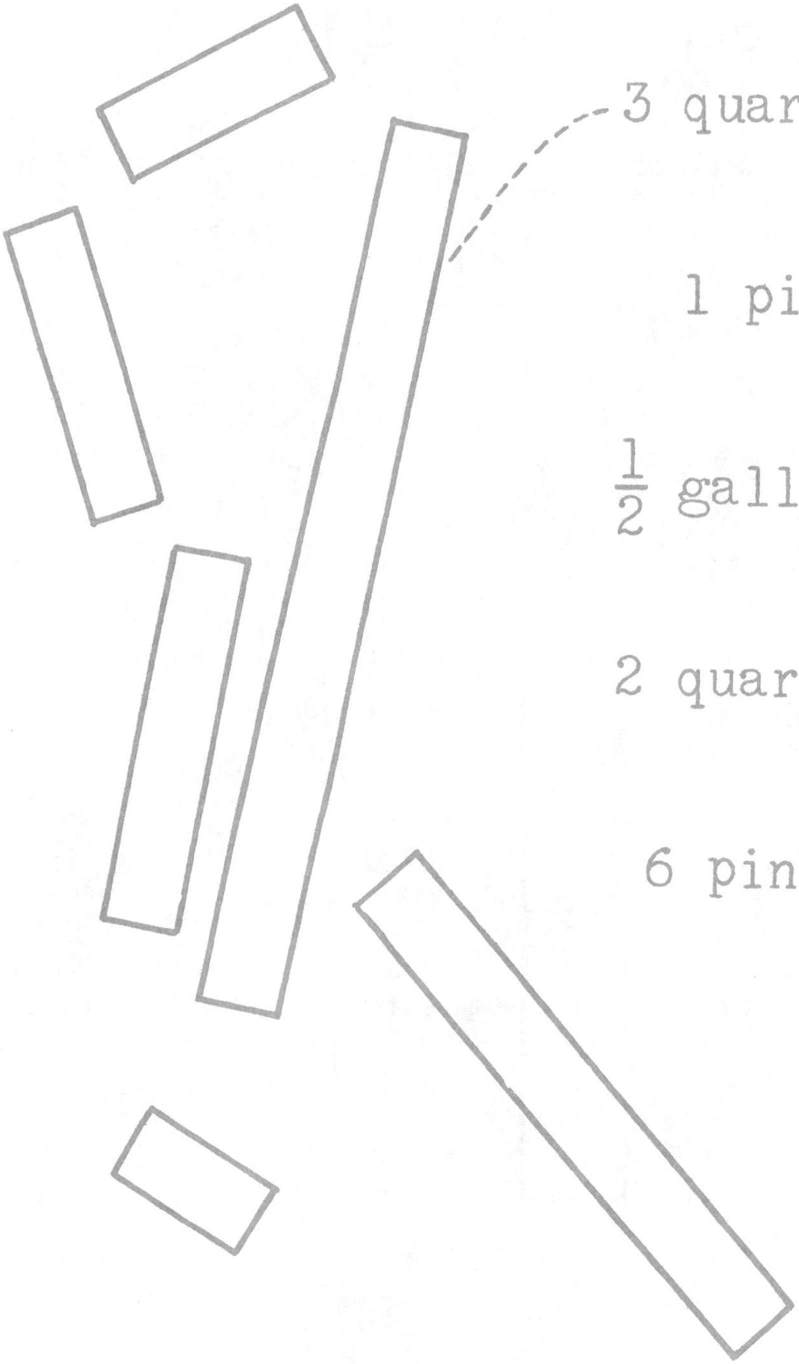

3 quarts

1 pint

$\frac{1}{2}$ gallon

2 quarts

6 pints

©1964 Lore Rasmussen

Ref: *Lab Sheet Annotations*, page 299.

Name ______________________________ Date ______________________

GALLONS	QUARTS	PINTS	CUPS
 →	4 →	→	
4 ←	 →	→	
←	←	 →	
←	←	←	

©1964 Lore Rasmussen

Ref: *Lab Sheet Annotations*, pages 299 and 300.

Name ______________________ Date ______________________

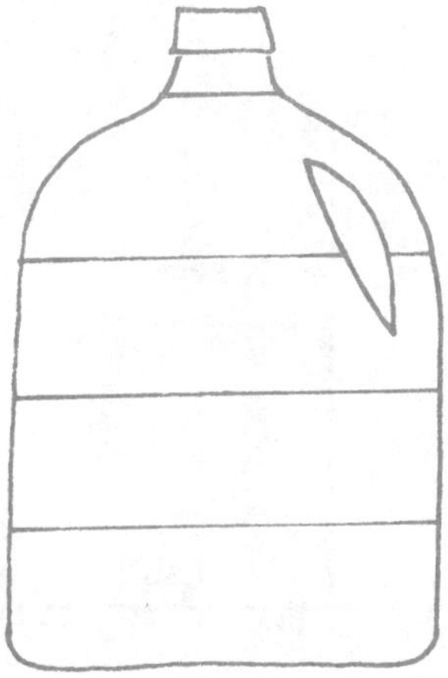

Put 2 quarts into the gallon jug. The jug is now $\frac{\square}{\square}$ full.

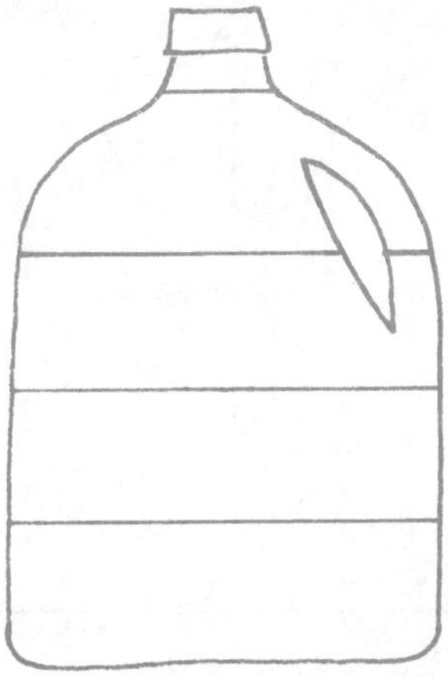

Put 16 cups into the gallon jug. The jug is now $\frac{\square}{\square}$ full.

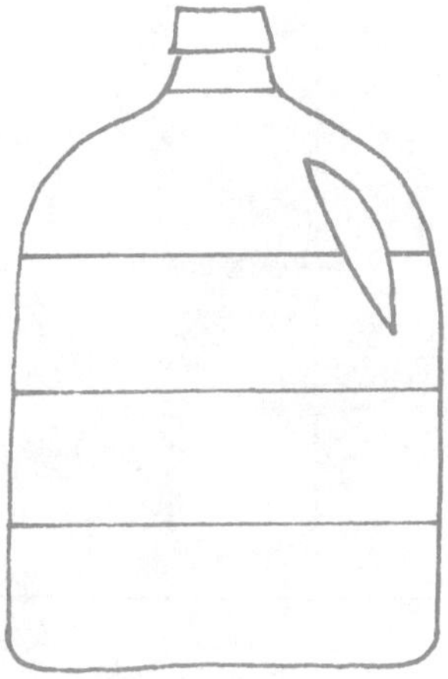

Put 2 pints into the gallon jug. The jug is now $\frac{\square}{\square}$ full.

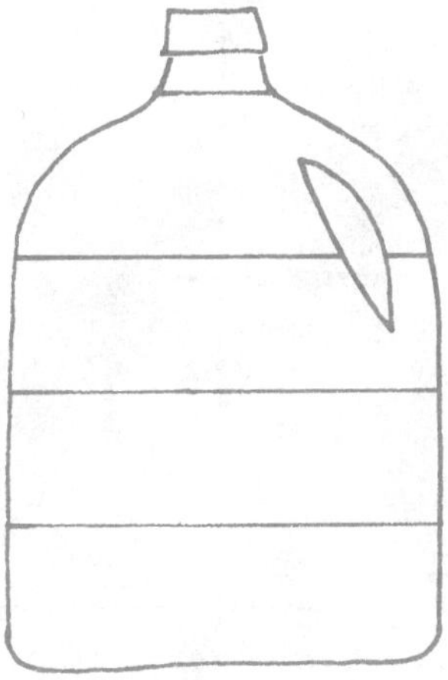

Put 1 quart, 2 pints, and 4 cups into the gallon jug. The jug is now $\frac{\square}{\square}$ full.

©1978 Lore Rasmussen

Ref: *Lab Sheet Annotations*, pages 299 and 300.

Name ______________________________ Date ______________

of a gallon

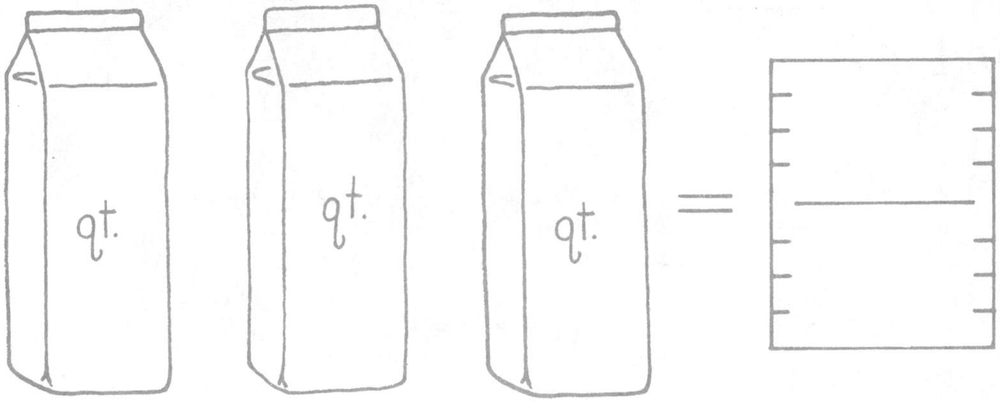

of a gallon

of a gallon

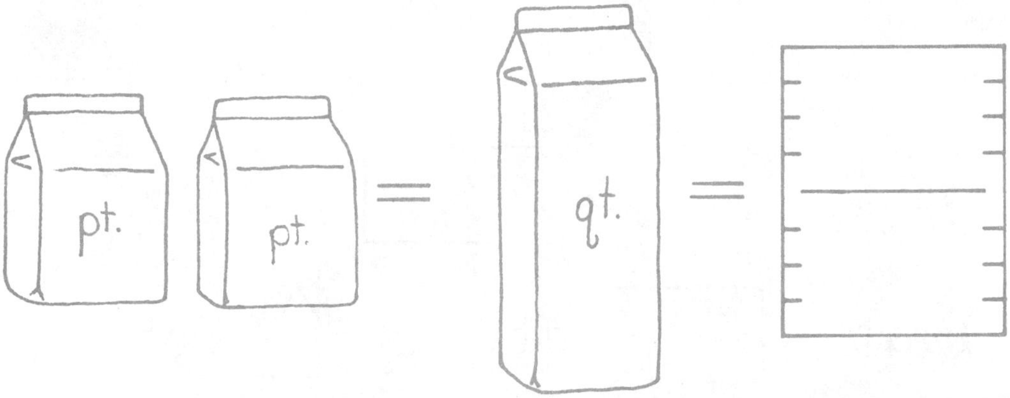

of a gallon

of a gallon

©1978 Lore Rasmussen

Ref: *Lab Sheet Annotations*, pages 299 and 300.

Name______________________ Date________________

gallons	quarts	pints	cups
gal.	qt.	pt.	c.

3 X 1 gal.= ☐ gal.

$\frac{1}{4}$ X 1 gal.= ☐ gal.

3 pt. = 1 qt.+ ☐ pt.

3 c. + 1 c.= ☐ c. = ⬡ pt. + 1c.

3 pt.	5 gal.	6 c.
+2 pt.	-4 gal.	+2 c.

8 c. = 3 c. + ☐ c.

7 qt. − 6 qt.= ☐ qt. = △ pt.

2 X 4 gal.= ☐ gal. = ⬡ qt.

3 gal. − 3 gal.= ☐ gal.= △ pt.= ⬡ c.

©1964 Lore Rasmussen

Ref: *Lab Sheet Annotations*, page 299.

Name ______________ Date ______________

Triangular Numbers

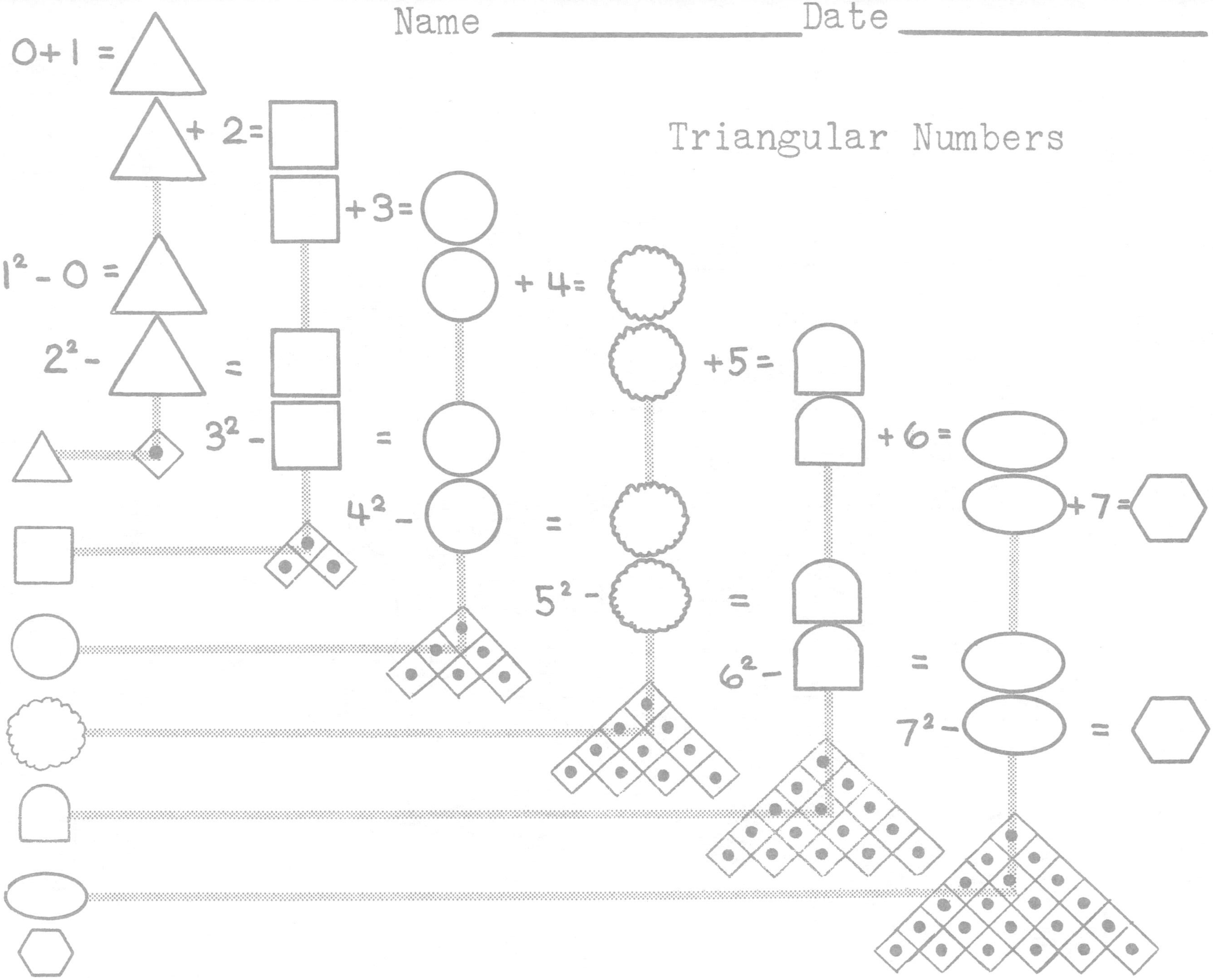

©1964 Lore Rasmussen

Ref: *Lab Sheet Annotations*, page 309.

Name ____________________ Date ____________________

A SPECIAL KIND OF TRIANGLE

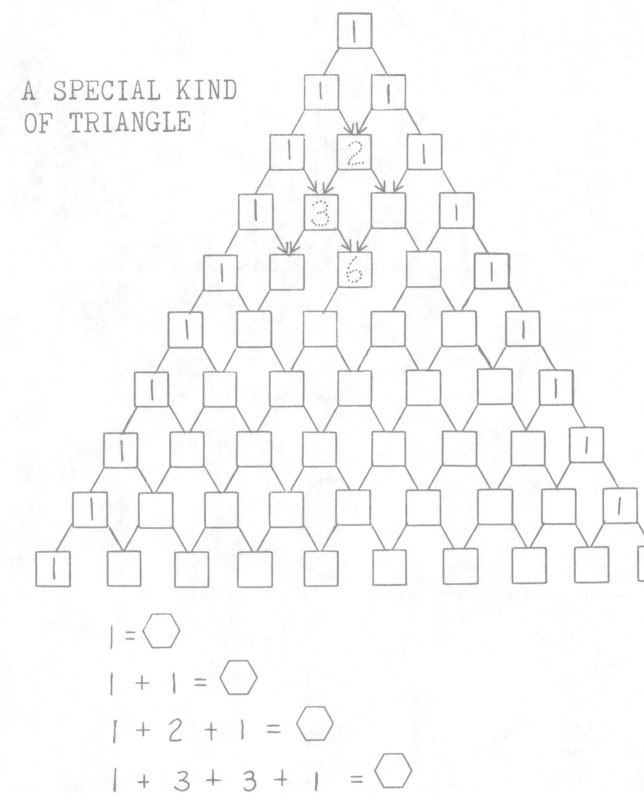

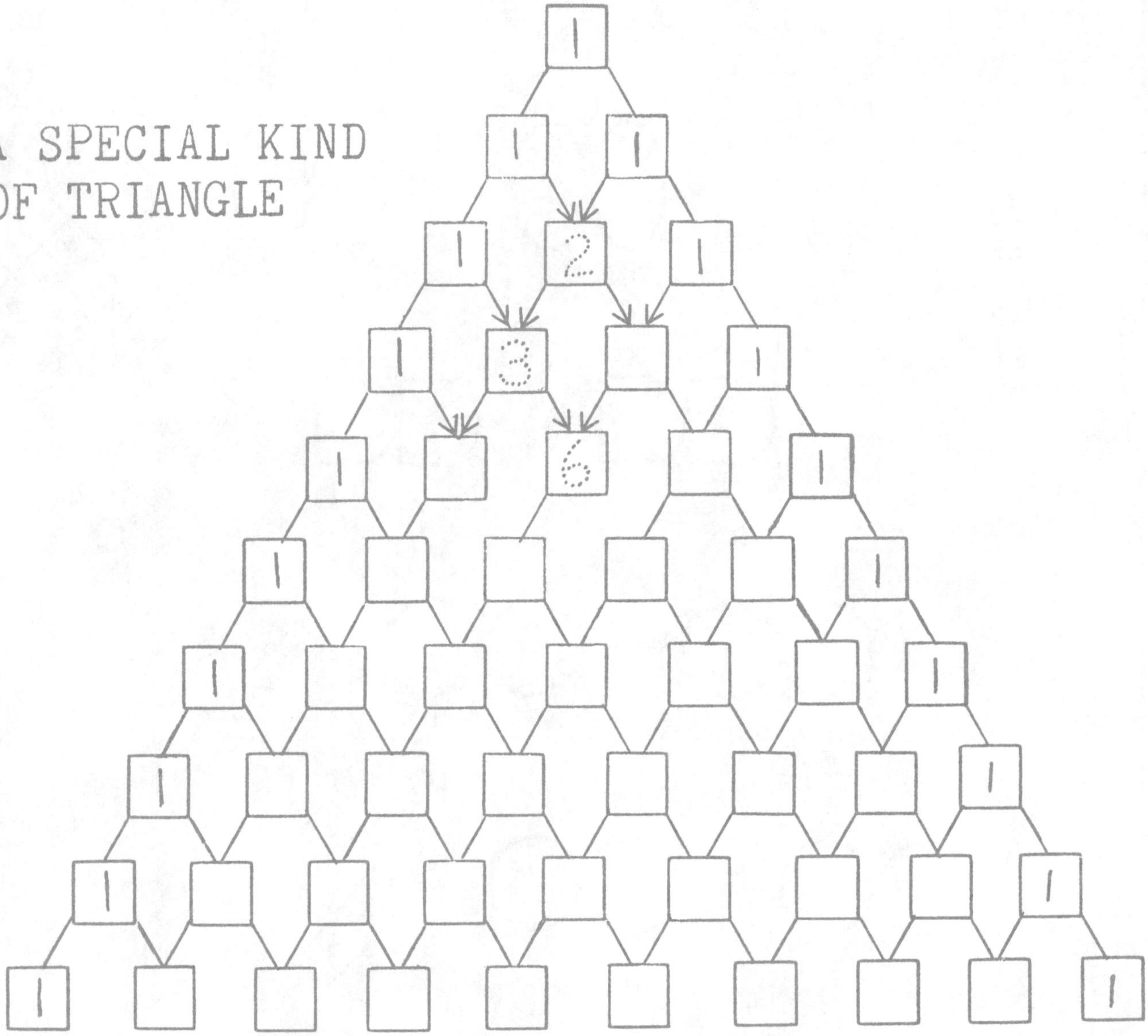

1 = ⬡

1 + 1 = ⬡

1 + 2 + 1 = ⬡

1 + 3 + 3 + 1 = ⬡

1 + 4 + 6 + 4 + 1 = ⬡

____ + ____ + ____ + ____ + ____ + ____ = ⬡

©1964 Lore Rasmussen

Ref: *Lab Sheet Annotations*, page 309.

Name ______________________ Date ______________________

In the ○ goes the difference between the two ◇ numbers above.

In the □ goes the difference between the two ○ numbers above.

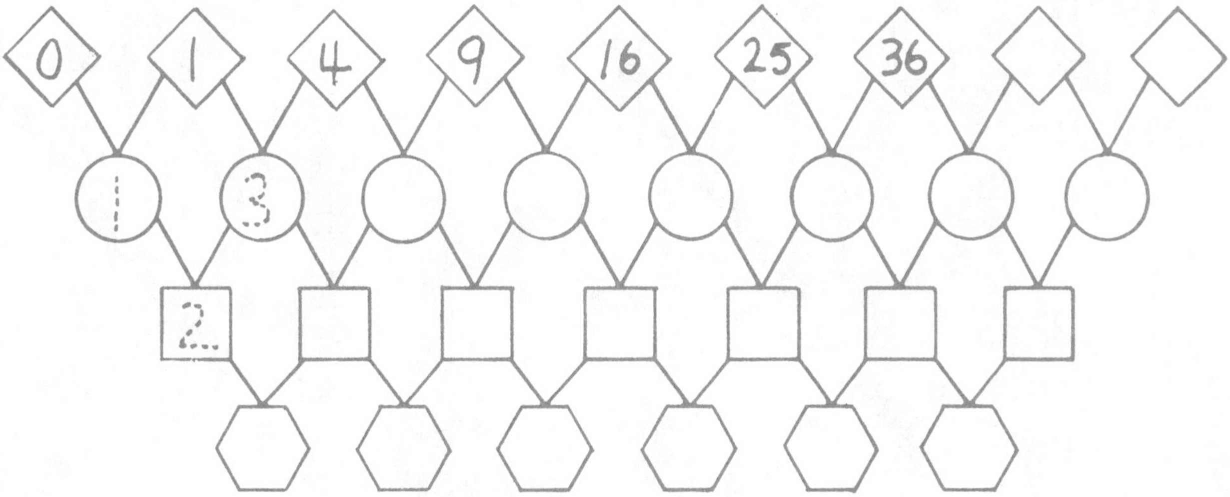

row 1

row 2

row 3

row 4

row A

row B

row C

row D

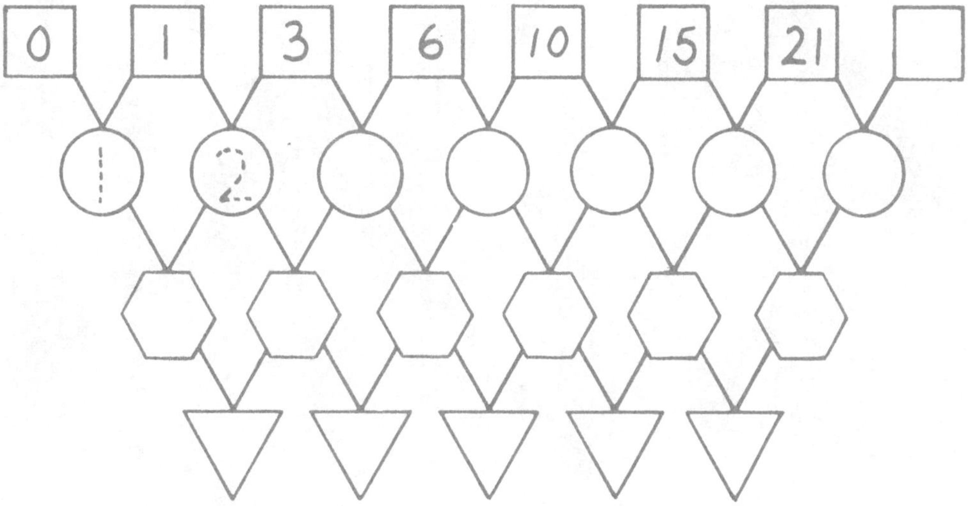

Each row has a set of special numbers in it.

Odd numbers are in row ______.

Triangle numbers are in row ______.

Square numbers are in row ______.

Counting numbers are in row ______.

Row 4 and row D have only ______________ in them.

©1964 Lore Rasmussen

Ref: *Lab Sheet Annotations*, page 310.

Name ______________________

Date ______________________

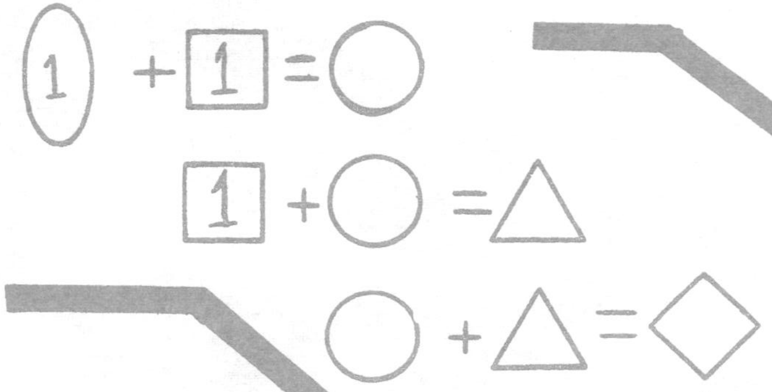

Find the Frame Numbers.

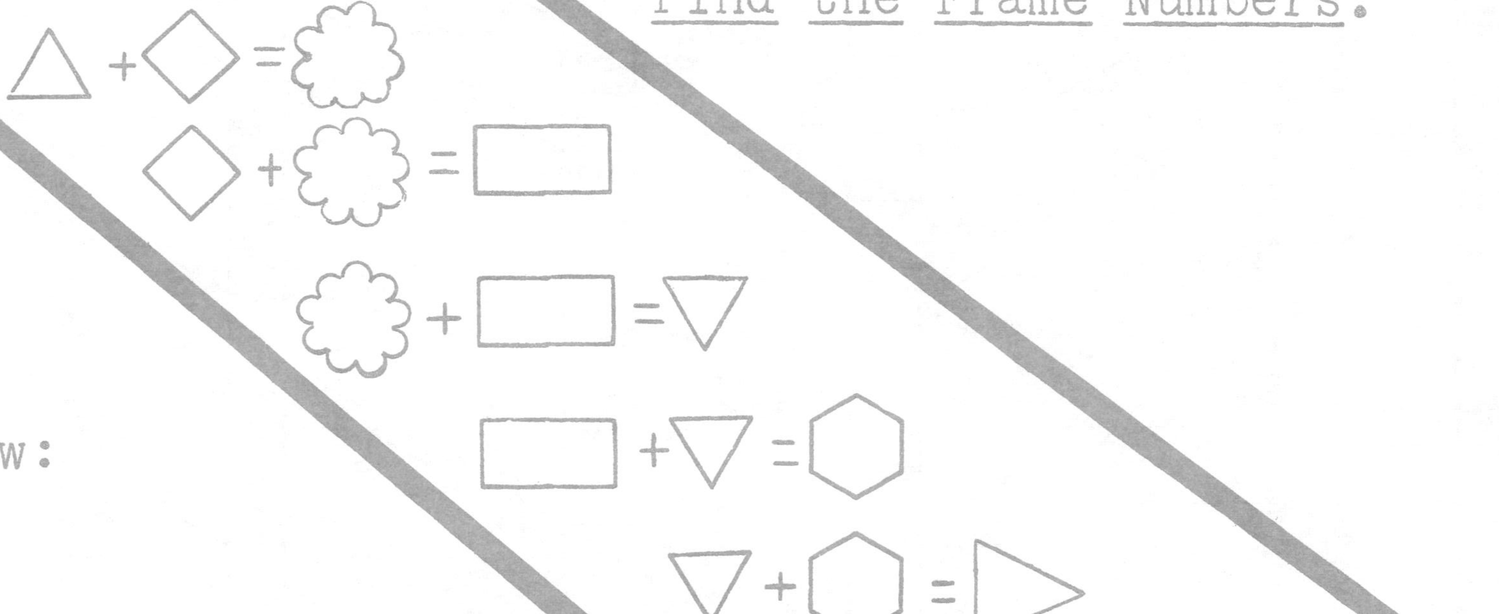

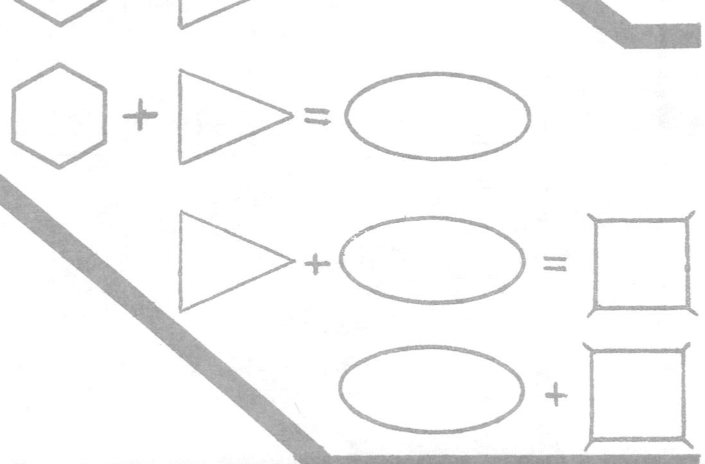

Fill in

the list of

frames below:

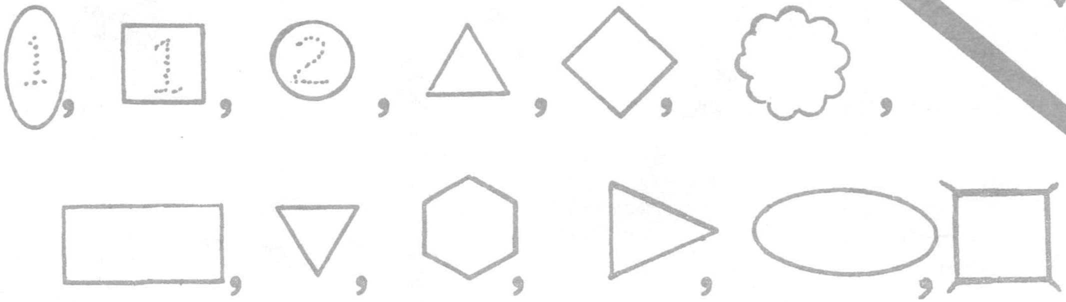

Ref: *Lab Sheet Annotations*, page 310.

©1964 Lore Rasmussen

Name ______________________ Date ______________

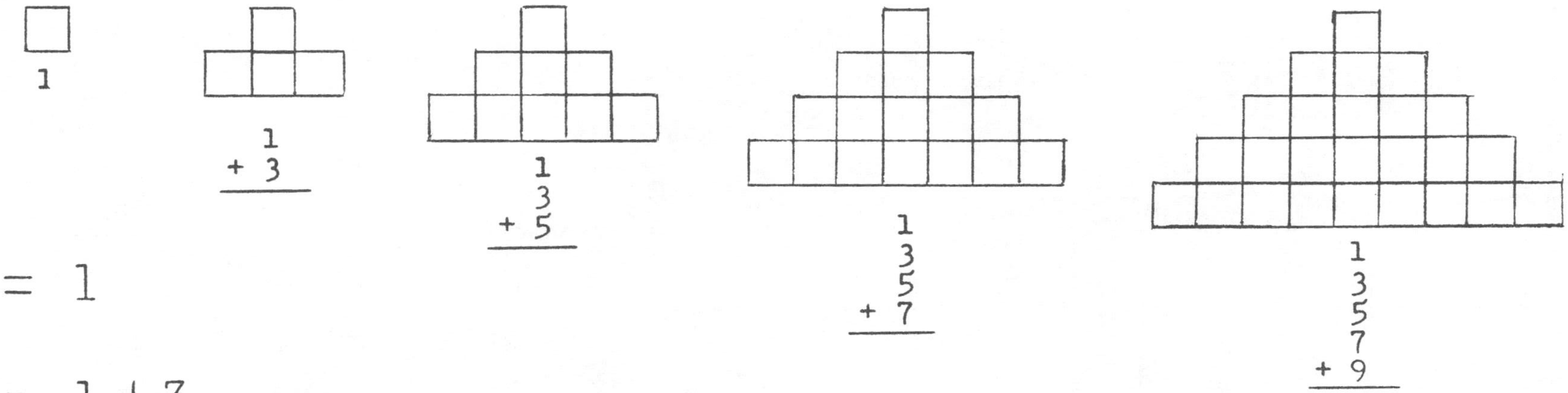

☐ = 1

☐ = 1 + 3

☐ = 1 + 3 + 5

☐ = 1 + 3 + 5 + 7

☐ = 1 + 3 + 5 + 7 + 9

☐ = 1 + 3 + 5 + 7 + 9 + 11

☐ = 1 + 3 + 5 + __ + __ + __ + __

☐ = __ + __ + __ + __ + __ + __ + __ + __

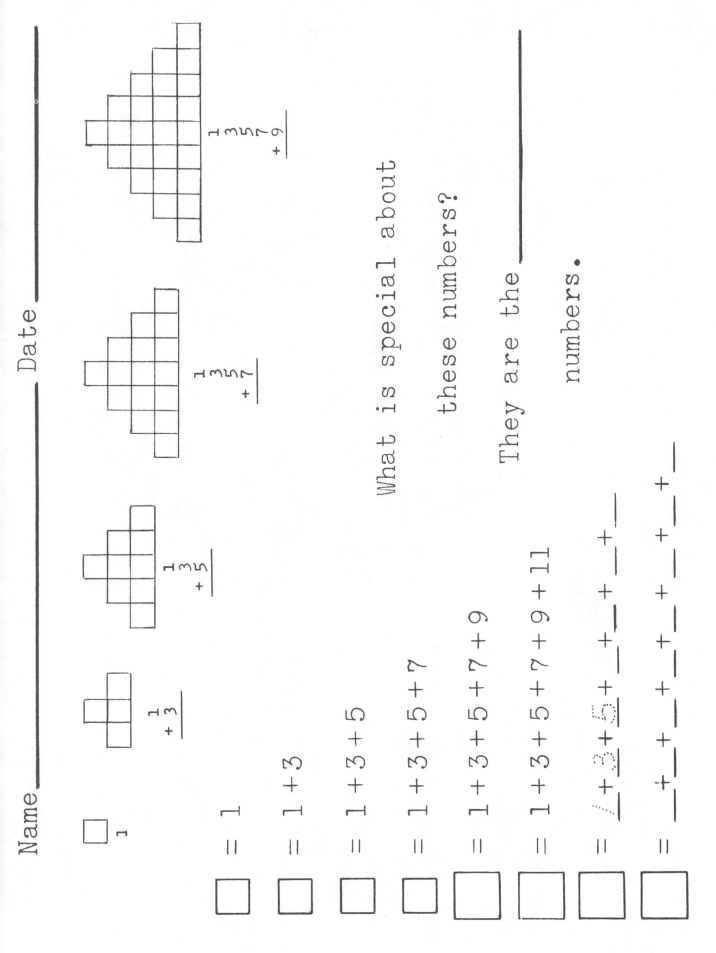

What is special about these numbers?

They are the ______________ numbers.

©1964 Lore Rasmussen

Ref: *Lab Sheet Annotations*, page 311.

Name ______________________ Date ______________

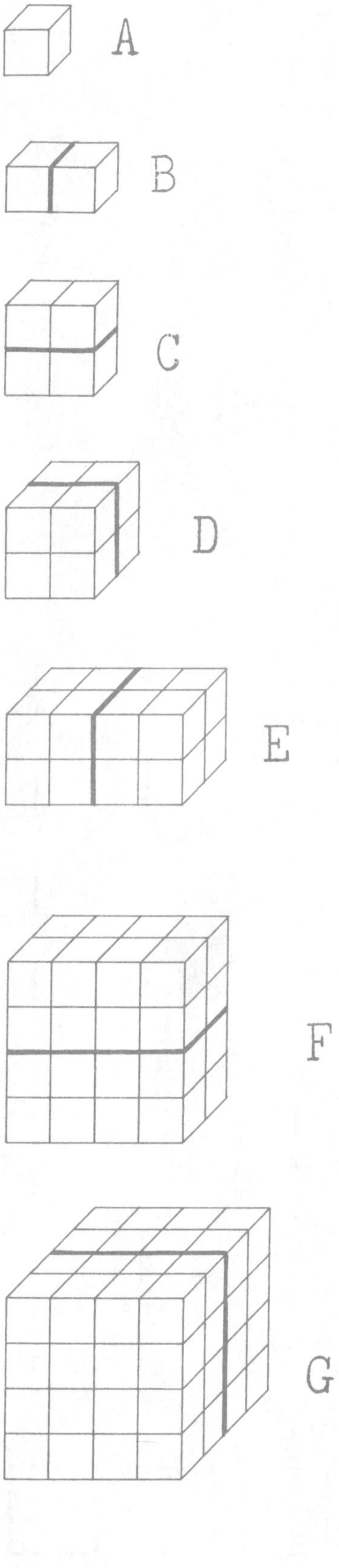

☐ , ☐ , ☐ ,
A B C

☐ , ☐ , ☐ ,
D E F

☐ , ☐ , ☐
G

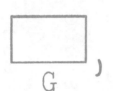

What is special about these numbers?

☐ = 1

☐ = 1 X 2

☐ = 1 X 2 X 2

☐ = 1 X 2 X 2 X 2

☐ = 1 X 2 X 2 X 2 X 2

☐ = 1 X 2 X 2 X 2 X 2 X 2

☐ = 1 X 2 X 2 X 2 X 2 X 2 X 2

©1978 Lore Rasmussen

Ref: *Lab Sheet Annotations*, page 311.

Name_____ Date_____

This footprint was
found on the beach.

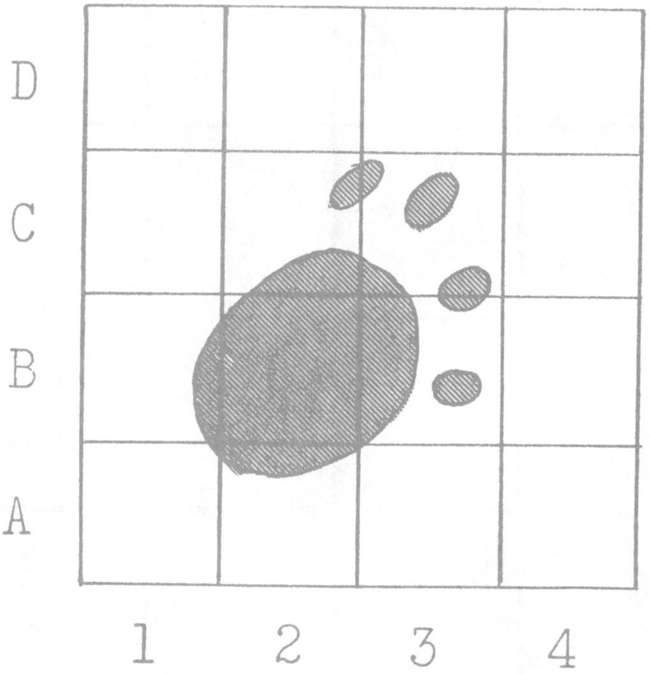

Make a small
picture of the
footprint.

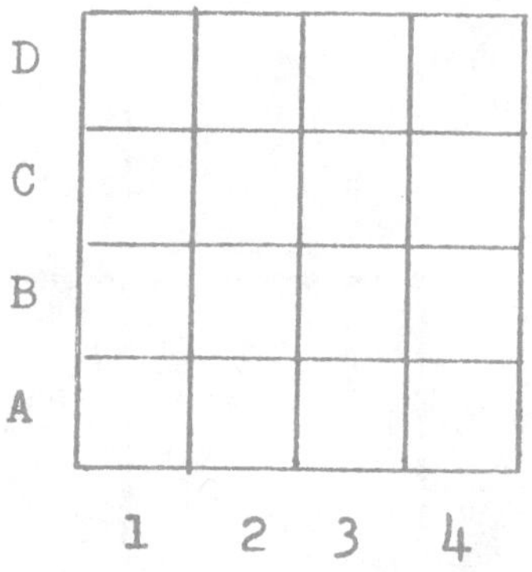

A small
doll's dress.

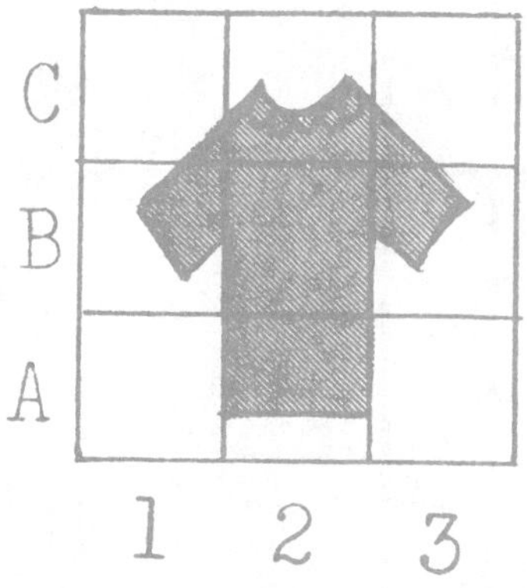

Make a dress like
it for a big doll.

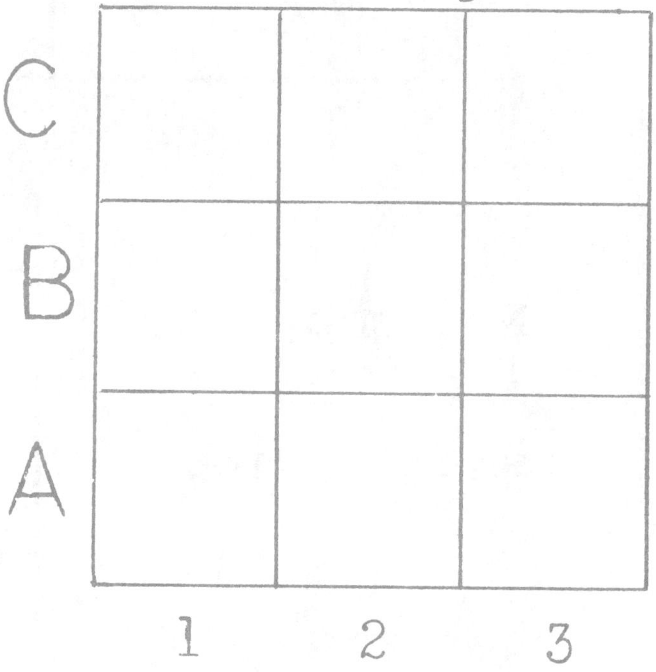

©1978 Lore Rasmussen   Ref: *Lab Sheet Annotations*, page 326.   ●●●● W-1

Name ______ Date ______

Trace your own hand.

F						
E						
D						
C						
B						
A						
	1	2	3	4	5	6

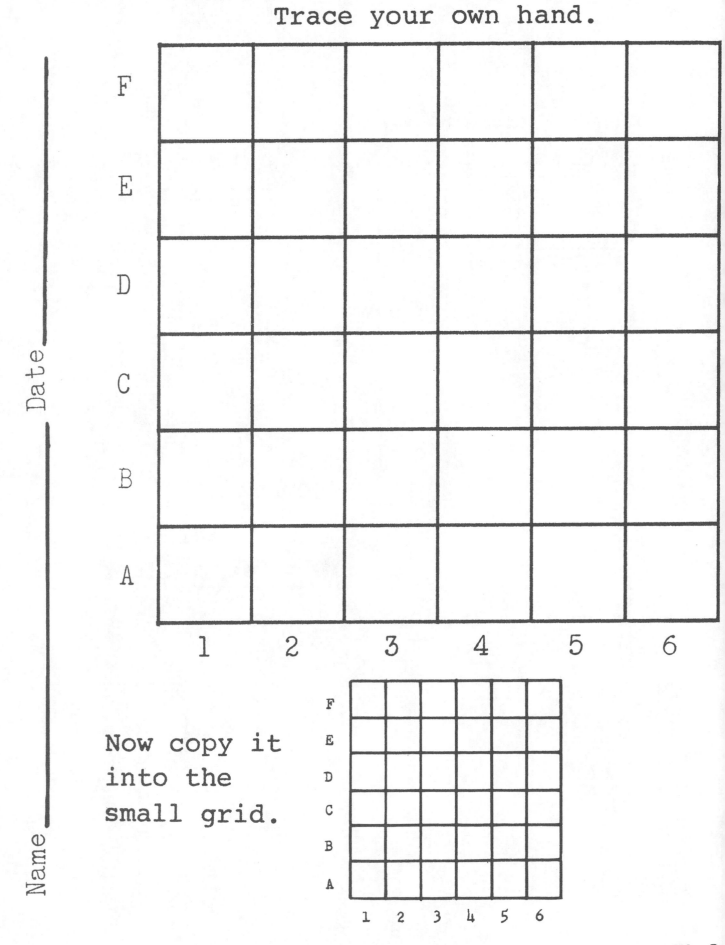

Now copy it into the small grid.

F						
E						
D						
C						
B						
A						
	1	2	3	4	5	6

©1978 Lore Rasmussen

Ref: *Lab Sheet Annotations*, page 326.

Name ______________________ Date ______________

A picture of a tree is mapped on Grid I.

We started the picture on Grid II. Finish it.

Map the picture on Grid III and on Grid IV.

Grid I

Grid II

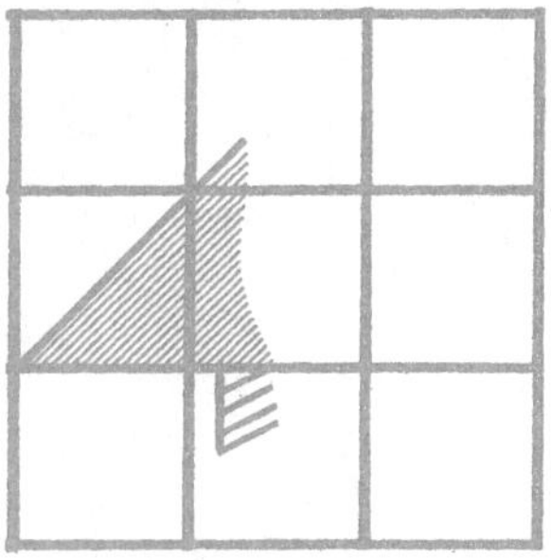

Grid III

Grid IV

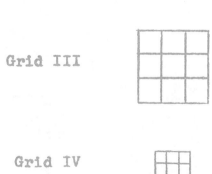

©1964 Lore Rasmussen

Ref: *Lab Sheet Annotations*, page 327.

Name__________________________ Date______________

A picture of a <u>duck</u> is mapped on Grid I and Grid II.

- First, finish mapping the picture on Grid III.
- Now map the picture on Grid IV.

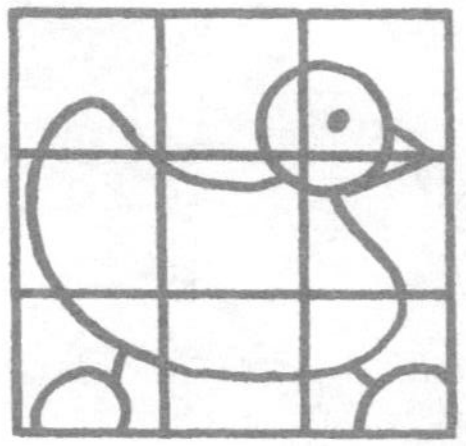

Grid I

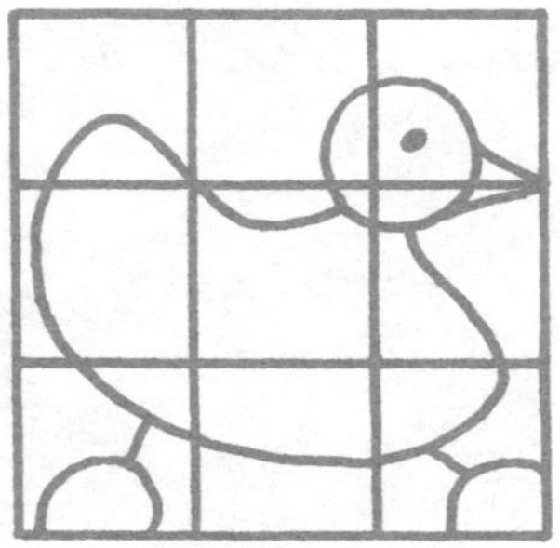

Grid II

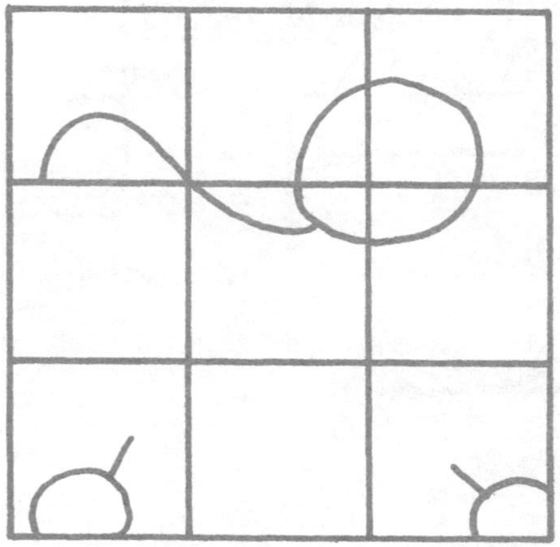

Grid III

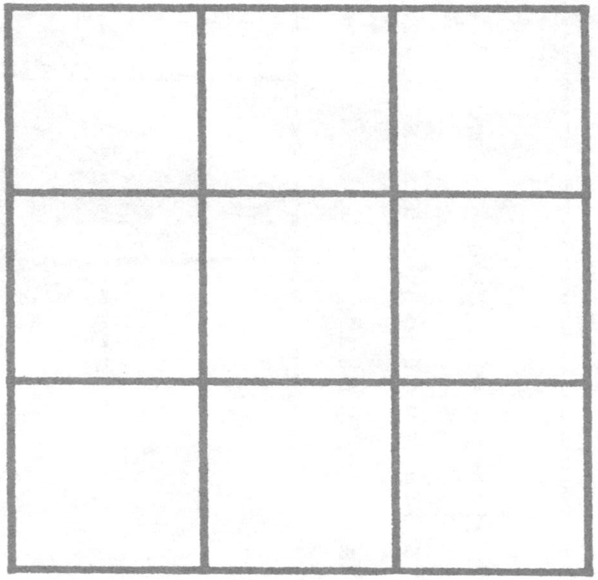

Grid IV

©1964 Lore Rasmussen

Ref: *Lab Sheet Annotations*, page 327.

Name ________________________ Date ________________

What happened to the Man?

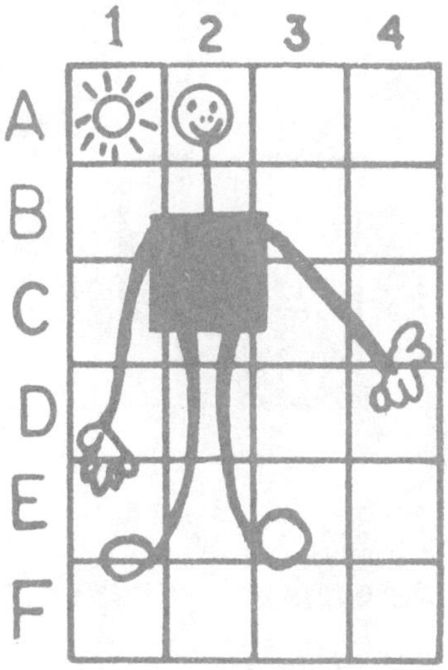

Grid I

Here he is.

Grid II

Oops!

We forgot something.

Draw in what is missing.

Grid III

Where are the eyes?

Draw them in.

What else is missing?

Where is the man?

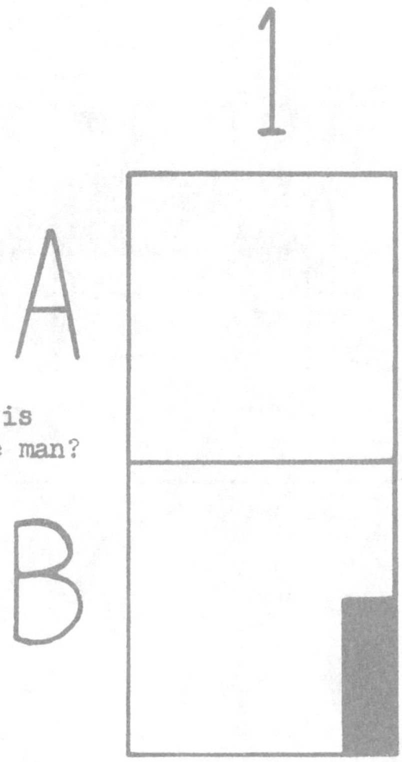

Grid IV

Draw in what's missing.

©1964 Lore Rasmussen

Name______________________________ Date____________________

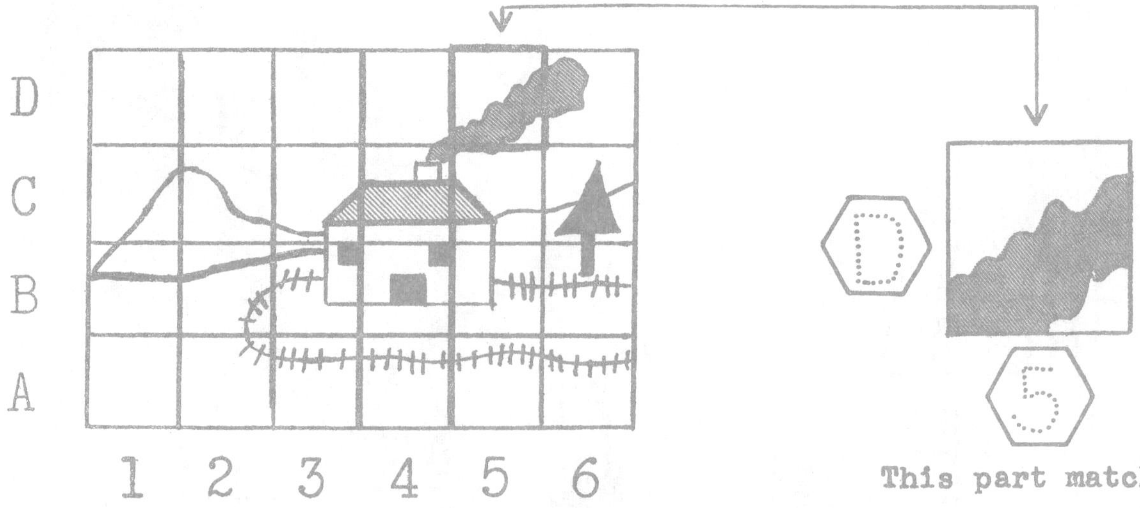

This part matches

D-5 in the picture.

Here are parts of the picture above.

They are made larger.

Match each part with the picture.

Label the parts.

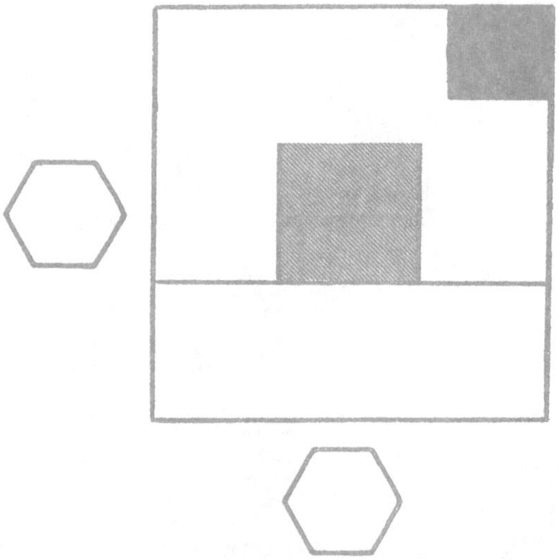

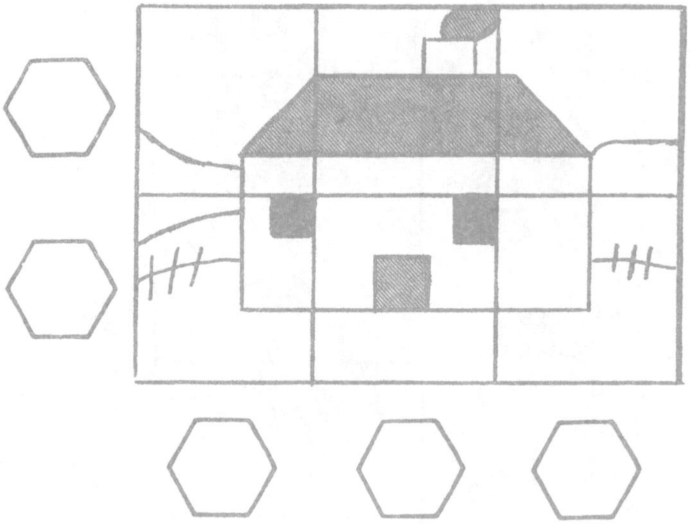

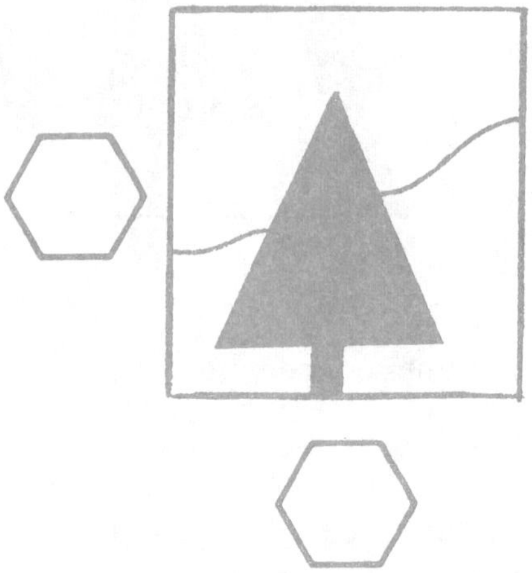

©1964 Lore Rasmussen

Ref: *Lab Sheet Annotations*, page 328.

Name ______________________ Date ______________

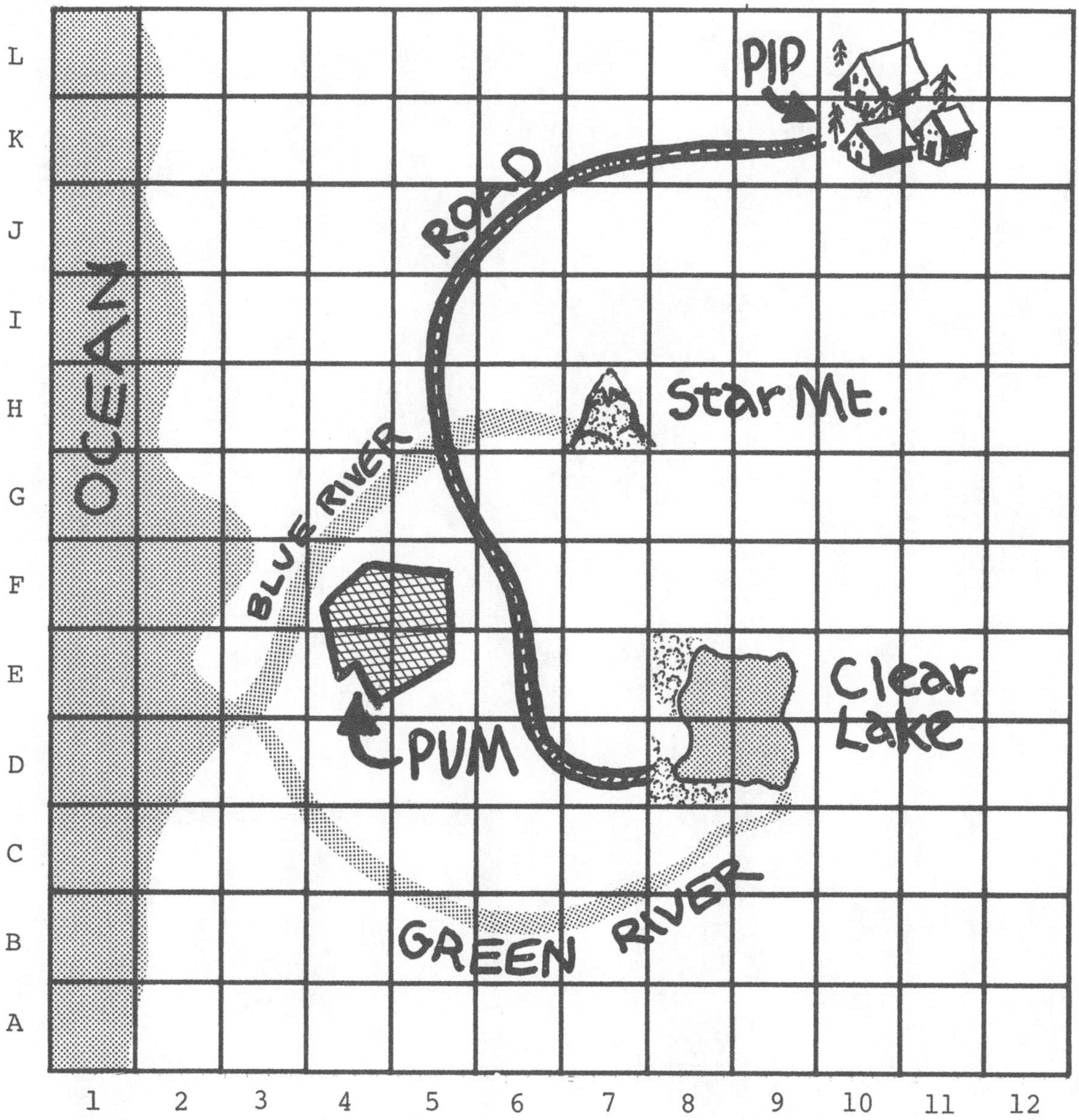

PUM is at E-4, E-5, F-____, and ____.

PIP is at K-10, K-____, L-____, and ____.

Star Mt. is at ______.

Clear Lake is at ____, ____, ____, ____.

©1978 Lore Rasmussen

Name ______________________ Date ______________________

You are going to make a map on page W-9.

T-2	T-3
S-2	

Park City is at

T-2, T-3, and S-2.

It is shaded in on the map.

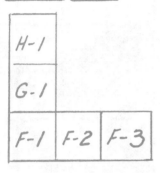

Big Town is at:

T-8	T-9	T-10	T-11
S-8	S-9	S-10	S-11
R-8	R-9	R-10	
		Q-10	
		P-10	

Shade it in on the map.

Little Town is at:

H-1		
G-1		
F-1	F-2	F-3

Shade it in on the map.

Ghost Town is at:

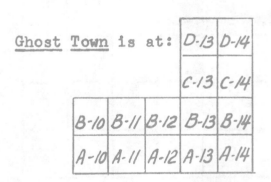

			D-13	D-14
			C-13	C-14
B-10	B-11	B-12	B-13	B-14
A-10	A-11	A-12	A-13	A-14

Shade it in on the map.

Make a **road** from A-1 to P-10.

Make a **highway** from R-10 to R-13; and from R-13 to D-13.

Blue Lake is at:

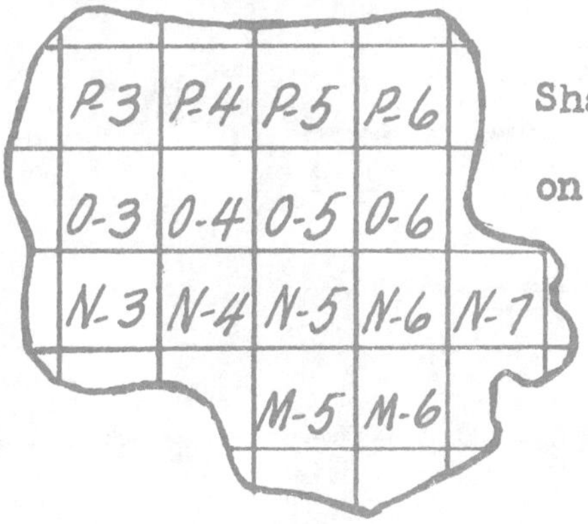

Shade it in on the map.

©1984 Lore Rasmussen

Ref: *Lab Sheet Annotations*, page 329.

Name ____________________ Date ____________

	1	2	3	4	5	6	7	8	9	10	11	12	13	14	15
T		PARK													
S		CITY													
R															
Q															
P															
O															
N															
M															
L															
K															
J															
I															
H															
G															
F															
E															
D															
C															
B															
A															
	1	2	3	4	5	6	7	8	9	10	11	12	13	14	15

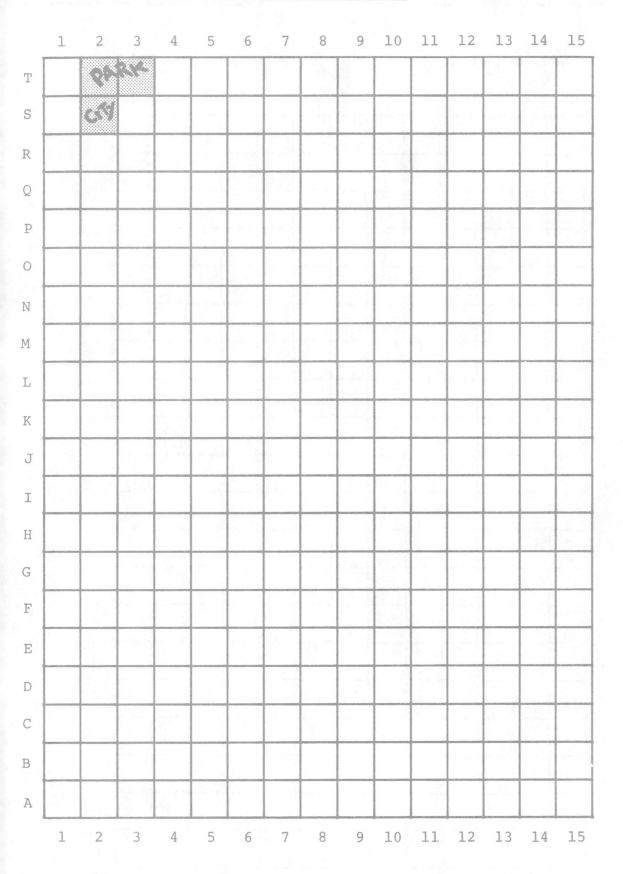

©1984 Lore Rasmussen

Ref: *Lab Sheet Annotations*, page 329.

Name________________________________ Date____________________

Make your own map on this grid.

	1	2	3	4	5	6	7	8	9	10	11	12	13
T													
S													
R													
Q													
P													
O													
N													
M													
L													
K													
J													
I													
H													
G													
F													
E													
D													
C													
B													
A													
	1	2	3	4	5	6	7	8	9	10	11	12	13

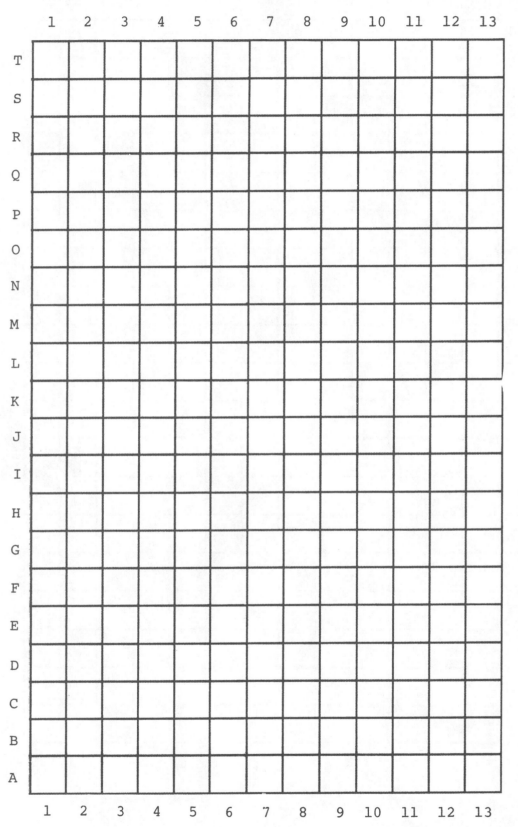

©1964 Lore Rasmussen

Ref: *Lab Sheet Annotations*, page 329.

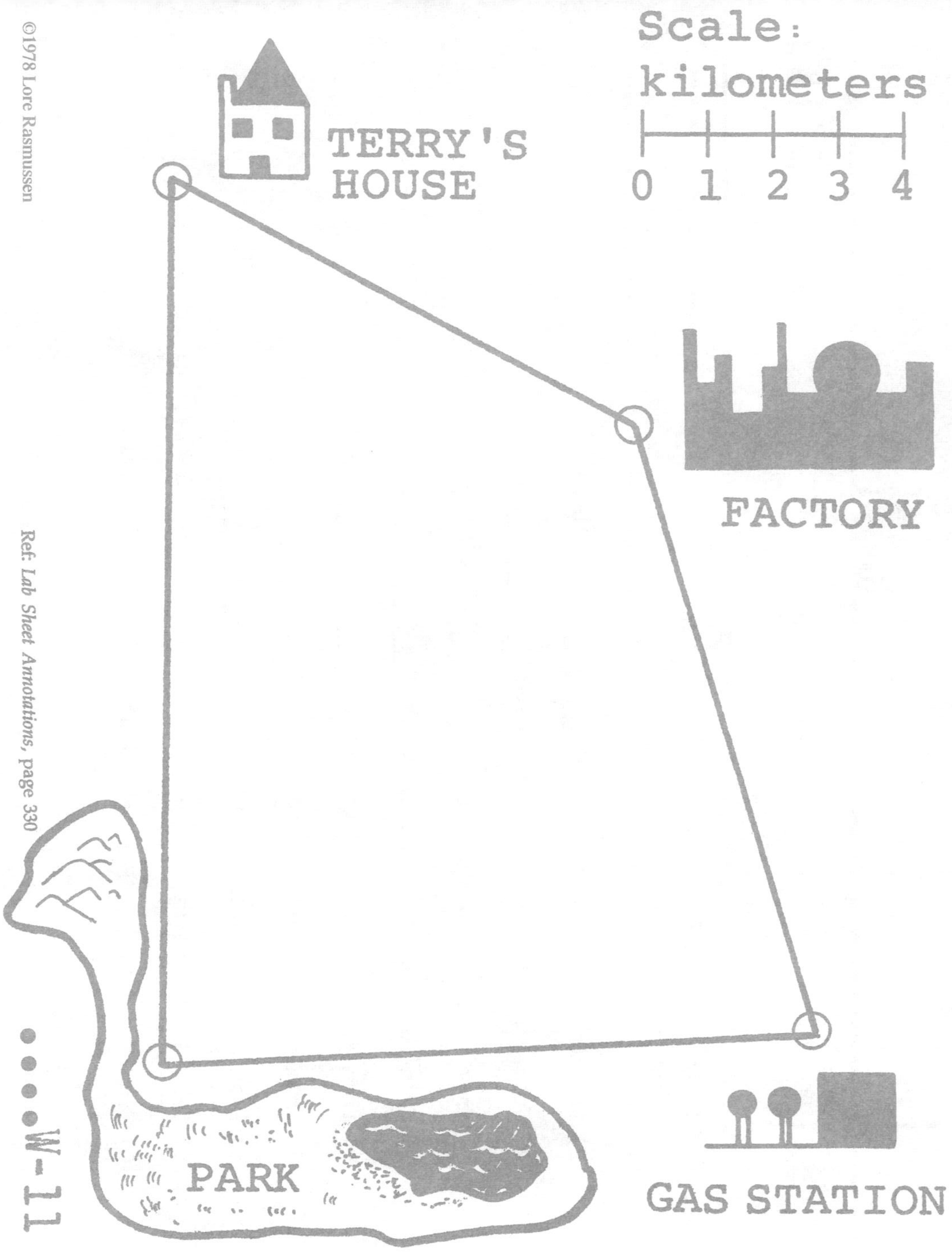

Name ____________

Date ____________

Use rods or a centimeter ruler.

The road from Terry's house to the park is ________ kilometers.

The road from the factory to the gas station is ________ kilometers.

The road from Terry's house to the factory is ________ kilometers.

The SHORTEST way from Terry's house to the gas station is ________ kilometers.

The SHORTEST way from the factory to the park is ________ kilometers.

©1978 Lore Rasmussen

Ref: *Lab Sheet Annotations*, page 330

Name ____________________

Date ____________________

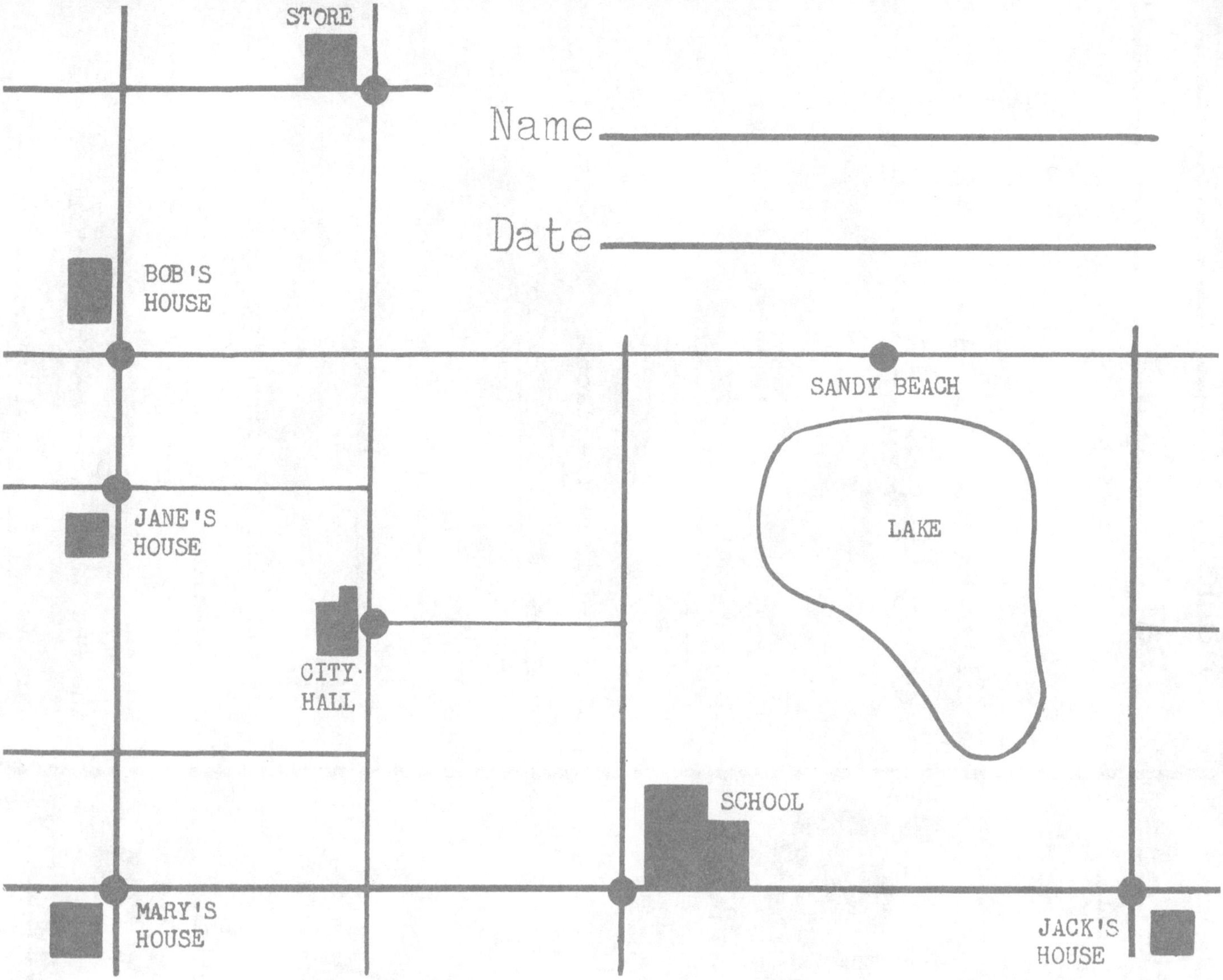

How far is the SHORTEST way:

1) from Jack's house to school? __________ blocks.

2) from City Hall to the store? __________ blocks.

3) from Bob's house to Mary's house? __________ blocks.

4) from school to City Hall? __________ blocks.

5) from Bob's house to Sandy Beach? __________ blocks.

6) from Mary's house to Sandy Beach? __________ blocks.

7) from Jane's house to Bob's house? __________ blocks.

8) from Mary's house to Jane's house? __________ blocks.

9) from Jack's house to Bob's house? __________ blocks.

10) from the store to Mary's house? __________ blocks.

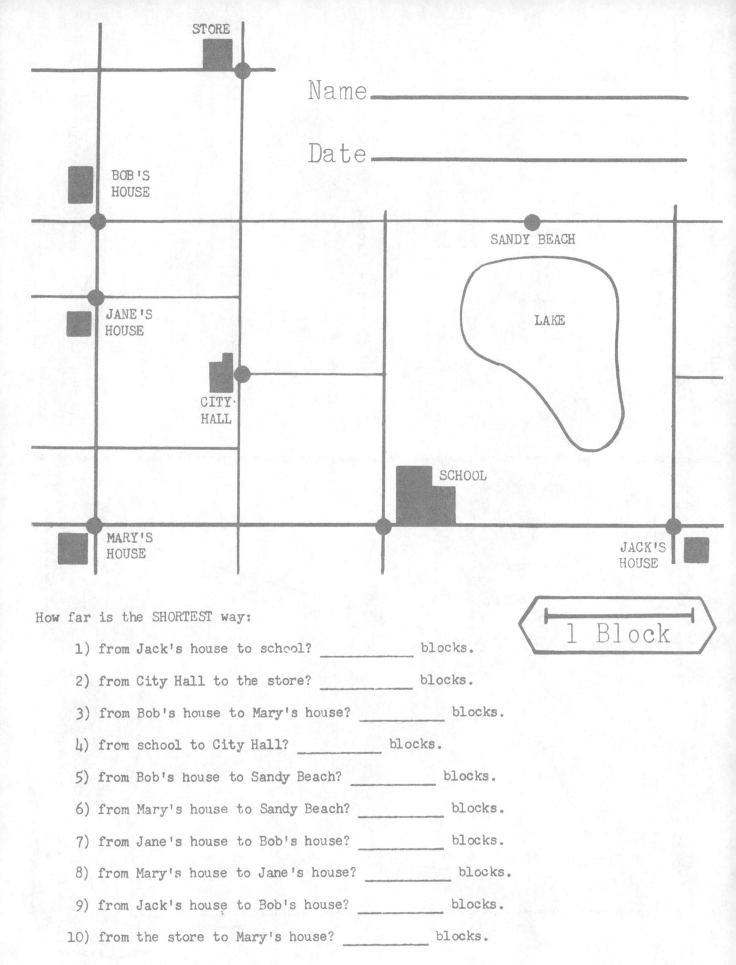

©1964 Lore Rasmussen

Name____________________ Date_______________

Telling Time

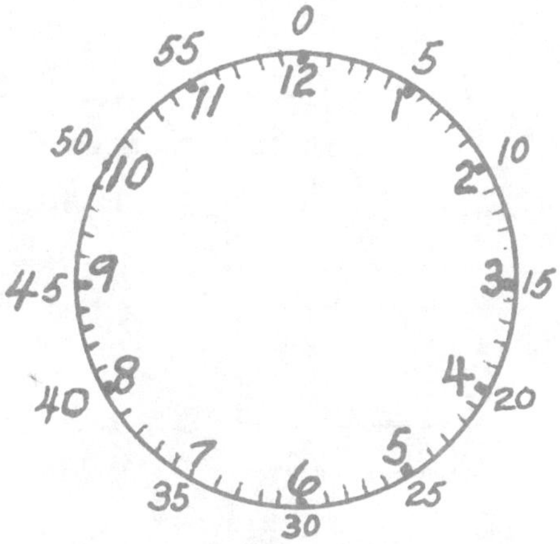

Five minutes ago	Now	In five minutes
12:10	12:15	12:20
	3:41	
	2:55	
	9:00	
	5:07	
	7:01	

10 minutes ago	Now	In ten minutes
10:10	10:20	
	4:17	
		6:00
	8:59	
4:48		
	11:50	

©1964 Lore Rasmussen

Ref: *Lab Sheet Annotations*, page 336.

Name ______________________ Date ________________

What time will it be half an hour after:

1:30 ☐

2:15 ☐

5:40 ☐

6:12 ☐

7:55 ☐

9:49 ☐

11:07 ☐

12:38 ☐

$\frac{1}{4}$ of an hour = ☐ minutes; $\frac{1}{4}$ X 60 = ☐

$\frac{1}{2}$ of an hour = ☐ minutes; $\frac{1}{2}$ X 60 = ☐

$\frac{1}{3}$ of an hour = ☐ minutes; $\frac{1}{3}$ X 60 = ☐

$\frac{3}{4}$ of an hour = ☐ minutes; $\frac{3}{4}$ X 60 = ☐

$\frac{1}{12}$ of an hour = ☐ minutes; $\frac{1}{12}$ X 60 = ☐

©1964 Lore Rasmussen

Ref: *Lab Sheet Annotations*, page 337

Name ______________________ Date ______________

Days and Weeks

Sun.	Mon.	Tues.	Wed.	Thurs.	Fri.	Sat.

Make a calendar.

The first day is a Tuesday. The month has 31 days.

One week has __________ days.

Two weeks have _________ days.

Four weeks have ________ days.

	Weeks	Days
10 days		
17 days	2	3
21 days		
26 days		
31 days		
35 days		
36 days		

©1964 Lore Rasmussen

Name ______________________ Date ______________________

Month		Number of Days		Number of Days and Weeks			
January	has	31 days	or	☐	weeks and	⬡	days.
February	has	28 days	or	☐	weeks and	⬡	days.
March	has	31 days	or	☐	weeks and	⬡	days.
April	has	30 days	or	☐	weeks and	⬡	days.
May	has	31 days	or	☐	weeks and	⬡	days.
June	has	30 days	or	☐	weeks and	⬡	days.
July	has	31 days	or	☐	weeks and	⬡	days.
August	has	31 days	or	☐	weeks and	⬡	days.
September	has	30 days	or	☐	weeks and	⬡	days.
October	has	31 days	or	☐	weeks and	⬡	days.
November	has	30 days	or	☐	weeks and	⬡	days.
December	has	31 days	or	☐	weeks and	⬡	days.
Add up the totals:		◯ days	or	☐	weeks and	⬡	days.

48 weeks and 29 days = ☐ weeks and 1 day.

There are ☐ months in a year.

There are ☐ weeks in a year.

There are ☐ days in a year.

©1964 Lore Rasmussen

Ref: *Lab Sheet Annotations*, page 338.